how to live with your
special
child

A PRACTICAL GUIDE FOR PARENTS and TEACHERS

PUBLISHED BY

acropolis books

WASHINGTON, D.C. 20009

how to live with your special child

A PRACTICAL GUIDE FOR PARENTS and TEACHERS

by George von Hilsheimer

FOREWORD BY **STEPHEN NEIGER, Ph.D., M.D.**

Appendices by

Hulda R. Clark, Ph.D. and **Sol D. Klotz, M.D., FACA, FAAA, FASI**

ACROPOLIS BOOKS
Colortone Building, 2400 17th St., N.W.
Washington, D.C. 20009

Printed in the United States of America by
Colortone Creative Graphics Inc., Washington, D.C. 20009

Type set in Times Roman
by Colortone Typographic Division, Inc.
Photos by Buckley Burton Paddock III
Design by Design and Art Studio 2400, Inc.

Library of Congress Catalog Number 76-114037

Standard Book No. 87491-309-8

The section on MODERN READING is
based on notes, comments and letters from
Hulda R. Clark, Ph.D., who developed
the system and by whom it is copyrighted.

foreword

George von Hilsheimer has selected me to write the foreword of his book. This is a great pleasure and a distinct honor. For the Rev. George von Hilsheimer is my friend and my teacher.

To say that the Rev. von Hilsheimer is my friend does NOT mean that we see eye to eye on all important questions, problems, and values of this life. To call him my teacher would NOT warrant the conclusion that I wish to practice everything he has to teach. Yet, both these words are used with deliberation—to introduce George as I see him, as one of the most stimulating and most unusual leaders I have ever encountered and one whose influence on my own personal and professional development was equal to that of no more than about half a dozen people. (And I have had several dozen teachers and friends who were far more famous and renowned than George is, including some who are Nobel Prize Winners and holders of similar awards.)

I met George about eight years ago on a dark, dark winter evening in snowy New York. I came, as usual, to attend interesting events and meet stimulating people. My host made me aware that George was speaking to a group that night. He felt that an evening spent listening to this provocative man would be just the right thing for the

6

visitor from dignified and dull Canada, America's frigid neighbor of the North.

It was an incredible evening all right. There was a stage, with a magnetic chap, impossible to describe in words, except that he was over six feet tall. At first I was struck only by some strong jokes in questionable taste (since then I learned from Paul Krassner, also one of George's friends, that the difference between freedom of speech and good taste often depends on "who is doing the free speaking and who the good tasting") which he used to underline his points and to polarize his audience of 200 or so young people: about twenty percent were enthusiastically for him, the remainder just as violently against him. (This, incidentally, turned out to be George's story of his life in all his other undertakings.) There I sat, perhaps the only member of the audience who was unable to decide if I was pro or con; not really because I was able to maintain my objectivity, but much rather because of my being paralyzed by the strong antagonistic forces acting upon me. For, you see, there was this unbelievable man, tossing out highly original, yet (to me) obviously true statements at the rate of about ten per minute; but doing so in a (to me) most offensive manner, and mixed among an equal number of "truths" I found myself unable to accept.

That evening turned out to be a model of my reaction to nearly every single project that has emerged from the incredible wealth and width (if not depth) of this equally incredible man's creative potential. Unfortunately, I have very little direct knowledge of some of George's adventures of which he is very proud, especially those originating before 1964. To my greatest regret, I did not see him and his group chase the KKK out of Miami, Florida with the help of .45 caliber pistols in 1954. I know little, except from indirect sources, about his dedicated work for black migrant farmers in 1961. I have similarly poor information about some of George's other activities, such as a restaurant he is supposed to own.

However, I do know a little (albeit not from direct evidence) about "Summerlane," which George proudly calls the first Summerhill type school in the United States. Although I have never seen this school, I almost became involved in its defense when I was told in 1964 that the New York State Board of Education attempted to close it. Having just barely met George (and not yet having seen any of his schools) I decided to prolong my stay in New York and spend a few days asking some of George's friends AND enemies, whether or not, in their opinion, I should become involved in this situation even to the extent of visiting the school preparatory to its defense. What George's FRIENDS said to me about the man at that time, had almost made up my mind that I better stay away from him and his school. Fortunately, I talked to his most dedicated ENEMIES (my friends in New York's middle class academic establishment) and they restored my faith that, by and large, George stands for almost all the things I also believe in, even if in his own peculiar way.

As it happens, I never saw Summerlane, because my testimony was not needed. However, my belief in George's integrity has increased over the years as our contacts intensified. In fact, I now consider George one of the most ethics conscious individuals I have ever met, even though I subscribe to a rather different ethical code than he does.

I can also bear witness to George's influence in my own fair city of Toronto, where he picked up a number of dubious characters (some with, and some without my help, in fact, some of the most dubious ones I met through George). However, these people then went on, inspired by George von Hilsheimer, to do some excellent work in the slums of Toronto, to pioneer a number of extremely original community projects and finally, to found a Summerhill Society in Toronto which, through a series of chain reactions, has since given birth to a number of most unusual educational experiments.

These educational communities, which were directly or indirectly influenced by George and his disciples, still exist. Regardless of how much or how little they approach my (or anyone else's) ideal of education (George himself has long outgrown them) they have certainly fulfilled the essential task of shocking the tired and formerly *ultra-conservative educational establishment of Toronto and Ontario into re-thinking their own philosophy of education and into attempting to come up at least with ever increasingly progressive statements and PLANS of new philosophies and methods since.*

Perhaps the above paragraphs will suffice to show my ambivalence towards George and most of his works. If so, I may be excused from elaborating on some of his other adventures which I witnessed, such as his role in the famous Ginzberg "obscenity" trial (Ginzberg MAY have lost even without having George on his side); or George's involvement in the manufacturing of extremely inexpensive experimental and applied psychological equipment (some of which even works).

I am considerably less ambivalent, however, towards what I consider George's major opus in life, Green Valley School —perhaps only because I know it somewhat better than his other accomplishments. Let me just say that, if there is anything very wrong with Green Valley, George has managed to hide it extremely skillfully from me, in spite of my visits there of one week's duration about twice a year.

Since Green Valley School incorporates all of George's crazy theories, I have not the faintest idea why it works. Perhaps it is because of these theories, perhaps it is in spite of them. Perhaps the secret of success is George's personality; or is it the climate and the abundance of palm trees, bamboo trees and other exotic flora on his 80 acre property; or perhaps the dedication of his staff; maybe a combination of all or none of these ingredients?

I can only report that each time I am down there I meet some psychologists and psychiatrists and other learned men from Daytona Beach, Miami (and even more far away places like New York) shaking their heads, having come ready to condemn this von Hilsheimer, but unable to do so when seeing some of the children whom they themselves referred just a few months ago to George. They were empty, burned out shells of human beings then, non-communicative near idiots, or hardened juvenile delinquents —what then trans-

formed them into live, inquisitive normal children again? They do not know and neither do I. I keep going to Green Valley because I have not yet given up hope that some day I may be privileged to find out.

The present volume, the way I see it, is meant as a summary statement of all of George von Hilsheimer's experience as an educator-therapist not only in Summerlane and in Green Valley School but also in his capacity as a consultant to a number of regular school boards. It is more than that; and I am not sure if this is too fortunate.

It is also a summary statement of all of George's philosophies and experiences. It is strong wine, new and intoxicating. It sounds like when a person, afraid that his first statement may also be his last, wanted to say all that is on his heart, regardless of direct or indirect relevance to his subject.

This is no reading material for the stickler for accuracy, for the person who is easily put off by sweeping statements and exaggerations. Right at the beginning of the book he will have to stand through some very persuasively described food faddism followed by all sorts of other unorthodox medical theorizing that is described as the gospel truth. (And, knowing George, no doubt it IS to him, at least at this stage of his life.)

However, even the chapters which strike this (rather conservative) reviewer as somewhat outlandish, contain an incredible wealth of productive theorizing, and much can be forgiven as long as it is viewed in this light: as just theorizing. Chapter one, "The Forgotten Flesh" reflects some of George's best Reichian traditions. Its emphasis on diet should be quite productive of further research. Indeed, some aspects of this have been tried with good results in some Scandinavian countries. His comments about the importance of sleep regularity are expressed with refreshing originality. The same applies to his views about the importance of structure, temperature, color, climate, biological rhythms and ecology of the teaching environment. (Have you heard of the British-Scandinavian "junkyard method" of teaching the building of a society?)

There follows a sub-chapter about psycho-kinetics, emphasizing

"TLC" (Tender Loving Care); the importance of easy touching (some of this theorizing has been put into effect in my own country in the Ontario Science Center designed especially for the touch of children); games and activities to encourage touching; tactics to increase identity and boundary awareness.

The pages on physical and emotional development, routines for physical development, (rich in concrete, original programs like "push away the sun," "partners squeeze") for relaxation and awareness, for enhancing contact, etc., (all full of classroom exercises—"feel the way your right leg fits into your body," "inhabit your foot," "feely-feely," "taste time," "blind," "deaf," "holding and freedom rooms") are in themselves worth many times the expense of the book—whatever it may be. The part on perceptual re-education abounds in examples that can be easily applied by any teacher in any classroom to create true adventures of learning for almost any child (and most adults, too). Emotional perception is an especially unique sub-chapter dedicated to the training (or re-training) in the awareness and expression of like—dislike, "feeling talk" and other "sunken continents" in the average North American man, woman and adolescent.

Chapters two, three and four are even more brilliant intellectual fireworks than chapter one. It is impossible to do justice to these chapters in a few pages. They are kept in similar style, somewhat complex theorizing, but expressed in powerful, short, easily comprehended sentences (this style is one of the great assets of the book) and illustrated with some simple examples in the integration of perception, motor communication and words; ("Try Dylan Thomas for the sonority of his voice. Do not explain or analyze. . . . Ask the children what they heard. . . . Push . . .) the creative use of creativity; ("How would a backward day be?") direct sensory contact; materials and plays that teach; the training in abstraction, (how would YOU like to see your favorite educational theory translated into the 800 words of basic English?) generalization and acute observation. There is a refreshingly original approach to the classical problem of teaching the "Three R's." (Can you use your fingers as an abacus?)

All along, von Hilsheimer continues to use some old and some revolutionary new teaching materials and techniques. They range from easy, self-constructed perceptual tasks to inexpensive reading instruction kits; from the uses of "moral honesty" (don't be detached; show your anger) and the "Man from Mars technique" ("MFM says no one ever fights on his world. How must they raise their children?") to "negative instruction," "negative practice" ("now I want you to disrupt the class") and tape, video, photo, movie and live "feed back" of students' own behavior (e.g., stop everything and do exactly what the child is doing). The Tom Sawyer effect is an enjoyable, original conceptualization.

"Terror Therapy," (the selective educational use of violence) while strong stuff for the "pseudo-progressive educator" is, in my opinion, theoretically sound and, as a form of moral confrontation, probably quite effective in the type of population with which Green Valley School has to work. However, I find "symbolic punishment" (e.g., a student wearing a sign "I am a big hero—I smuggle beer") more original and (in my experience) no less effective.

There is a series of eleven appendices which are only loosely related to the main theme of the book. They range from the completely relevant to the questionable, to the highly relevant and even the brilliant.

All in all, HOW TO LIVE WITH YOUR SPECIAL CHILD: A HANDBOOK FOR BEHAVIOR CHANGE, uneven though it might be in many places, should prove to be a goldmine for the creative educator. It is warmly recommended especially to the discriminating, experimentation minded superintendent and principal and the curious, adventuresome classroom teacher who is bored with routine.

I pray that the book's weaknesses be excused in the light of its far greater strengths. I fervently hope that through it, George may influence still more kindred spirits the way he already has inspired many—not to become slavish, sectarian followers of yet a new "ism"; (George would want this least of all) but to be inspired to critical and yet sympathetic and even grateful tryouts in careful application of (and research on) at least some of the millions of his ideas for their own professional growth and personal development.

June 1969
Toronto.

STEPHEN NEIGER, Ph.D., M.D.
Chief Psychologist
Etobicoke Board of Education

author's introduction

THIS HANDBOOK IS WRITTEN for people who work with people. It is written to help guide those working with children whose actions are in themselves unproductively dangerous, unpleasant, uncomfortable, or unwanted.

The handbook is merely that. It makes no attempt to display the scientific underpinnings of the procedures recommended, or to argue the case of behavior training versus analysis or therapy.

The handbook is based on the conviction that unwanted behavior can readily and effectively be changed, and that this is worth doing. Overwhelming evidence is available proving beyond doubt that isolated behaviors can be changed without fear of dangerous conflicts, substitution of even worse actions, or other demons that frighten analysts and others. This handbook is for teachers who would rather work with a dry disturbed kid than with a wet one. It is for teachers who have the compassion to see that ready relief from an embarrassing behavior is worth weeks of talk.

The handbook describes techniques aimed at enlarging self control. It is not a program for detailed control of others. It provides means for decongesting people whose lack of integration has left artifacts of external controls and experiences which cause unwanted and uncontrollable behavior. Few are the children who like wetting the bed. They wet the bed because of poor habits, regression under pressure, inattention, or perceptual and cognitive isolation from fleshly sensations and actions. If, in fact, a child wets the bed as a hostile act against his parents, the hostile act itself is self destructive and the child can be taught a more effective way of dealing with his parents after he has learned to stop wetting his bed.

My biases and goals are toward waking people up, increasing their awareness, loosening their roots, dissolving their armor, disinhibiting, decongesting, enlarging the field of their being—in short, making people more alive. This approach is based on a conviction that there are more appropriate human means of self control than by irrational automatic inhibition. The evidence is overwhelming that as people are freed from barriers to feeling and to action, their controls become more refined and their abilities enhanced. For example, we have found that promiscuous girls generally have very rigid, moralistic views about sex. We find that when they have become chaste, their sexual attitudes are more relaxed, less moralistic and rigid. (Criminologists generally agree that criminals are more, rather than less moralistic than the general population.)

These procedures have grown out of ten years of experiment and demonstration in programs initiated and operated by *Humanitas.* These programs have been directed to a wide range of human beings in North America—migrant farmers and their children; farm families; urban slum dwellers (both U.S. Negro and Canadian Anglo); Indian families on reservations and in cities; middle class families in city and suburbs; wealthy families; people in church, school, and remedial, rehabilitative, correctional and therapeutic institutions; and people in training for adult professional, volunteer and business programs. The range of success with these tactics has been 86 % with addicts and psychotics to 99% with school dropouts and failures.

Green Valley, a residential school for "children in trouble," operated by *Humanitas,* offers parents the return of their entire three year cost if a secondary student sent to them is not admitted to a "selective" college and does not do well there. Green Valley also agrees *never* to expel a child for any reason. Green Valley's student population includes psychotic, addicted and criminal children as well as former school failures. It has never had to refund a tuition fee.

I am satisfied that the techniques recommended in this handbook are the core methods of our success. While a few are most easily carried out in a residential setting, most have been refined in day settings. Many of our "day" settings include working with slum kids on the street without any facility at all, or working in a slum room, or in a store front. We have also worked in normal classrooms, and regularly train teachers for public school classroom work.

For the serious scholar, or the merely argumentative, let me point out that I have written a monograph, IS THERE A SCIENCE OF BEHAVIOR? Humanitas Curriculum, Orange City, Florida, 1967, in which the scientific underpinnings of the technology described in this handbook are thoroughly referenced (540, to be exact).

Let me also point out that Appendix IV will give parent or teacher a readily accessible source of supply for most of the devices and materials recommended in this handbook. Appendix XI closes with a brief bibliography which I highly recommend.

GVH

contents

19

children in trouble
SOME SIMPLE IDEAS

Some children are in trouble.

Some children in trouble repeat actions that
get them into trouble.

Most children in trouble live in neighborhoods and homes and go to schools where
many children do not get into trouble.

Some kinds of trouble that children are in:
*wearing unusual clothes, talking very
strangely, being dirty and behaving queerly,
but not really harming people or property;
this kind of trouble lies mostly in adults'
reactions, which are very constant and very hostile;*

doing poorly in school;

leaving school;

quitting work;

running away from home;

breaking laws;

using drugs or alcohol;

sexual misadventure;

physically damaging themselves;

*trying to kill themselves; some manage and
are no longer in trouble;*

none of these, but being very unhappy.

Most children in trouble are in more than
one kind, or soon will be.

Most children in trouble say that they are very unhappy.

Most children in trouble have very ordinary
ideas about what is right and what is wrong.

Most children in trouble think that they are bad.

Most children in trouble don't like themselves
   or anyone else.

Most children in trouble are bored and do
   not see anything to do; they don't know how
   to do much anyway.

Most children in trouble see little reason to
   be any other way.

Most children in trouble think they cannot
   change, and most adults they know agree with them.

Most children in trouble get serious attention
   from adults only by being in trouble.

Most children in trouble get no rewards for
   doing and saying nice things; their friends
   often punish them for staying out of trouble.

Most children in trouble do not know many adults.

Most children in trouble seldom are alone with an adult.

Most children in trouble do not know a happy adult.

Most children in trouble do not understand
   what the adults they know do as work.
   And they sense how many of the adults
   they know don't respect their own work at all.

Most children in trouble are usually told and
   told and told what they should do, getting
   quite different advice from different adults.

Most children in trouble do not know any
   adults who behave in the same way toward
   them most of the time.

Most children in trouble think all adults
   are inconsistent and hypocritical; and most
   adults they know in fact are.

Most children in trouble respond to talk
   about what they should do as if the talk
   itself were a punishment; yet most adults
   who say they want to change the children
   only talk to them.

CHILDREN IN TROUBLE NEED A CHANCE:

to feel that they are worth something;

*to think that they can change themselves
and some circumstances around them;*

to feel that change is worth making;

to develop skills and use them;

to know some adults who will listen to them;

to know some adults who will answer them courteously;

*to know some adults who see that work goes
beyond the children themselves, but who
are interested in the children;*

*to know some adults with many skills, and
who are strong enough to avoid trying to
appear perfect, controlled, and as if they
didn't need to grow more themselves;*

*to know some adults who behave toward
children with the same gravity, respectful
attention and lack of impertinence that
they would grant a friend in trouble;*

*to know some adults who will pay strongest
attention to them when they are doing
worthwhile things, and who are obviously
not interested in them simply because they are bad;*

*to know some adults who will tell them
"no" fairly, consistently, and with the
strength to follow through;*

*to know some adults who understand that
haircuts, fingernails, clothing and cleanliness
are trivial, while the important things are
concern for knowledge, self control and ability;*

*to know some adults who are strong enough
not to need to make children need them,
who can force children to make decisions
for themselves, and can help them live with
bad decisions and overcome them . . . thus
learning to make good ones.*

the forgotten flesh

I
THE VEGETATIVE FUNCTIONS

ABOUT 85% OF NORMAL AMERICAN MEN and 98% of normal American women suffer from readily diagnosed diseases causing loss of energy, discomfort or disability. These figures seem to be consistent for the British and Western Europeans. Most people are able to ignore the *dis*-ease caused by faulty biological processes. Many children are slow developers, suffer handicaps and disorders and yet give difficulty to no one. We can hope for a day when decent medical inventories are routine. These stronger characters will then maximize their abilities and enjoyment.

It is almost certain that a troubling child will have a disabling or uncomfortable medical disorder. His characteristic style of response to the people around him will almost certainly be built around those disorders. Even though we have known these fundamental facts for generations it is still characteristic for a child to be sent to a behavior specialist or a care center without his having had fundamental medical examinations. We are constantly amazed that children are almost never sent to us having had sophisticated eye examinations. Out of more than five hundred children sent to one of our centers in the last six years only one had been thoroughly tested for hearing. Not one was sent with a thorough developmental analysis, no diet surveys, fewer than twenty allergy screenings, one test for hypoglycemia, none even for worms, and very few routine thyroid function tests, blood counts, iron assessments or other readily indicated examinations.

We have found almost all of the children sent to us to be suffering from medical liabilities readily detectible by any teacher with the slightest awareness of her children, plus a three hour course in hygiene.

Simply removing disabilities will not teach a child to read. Treating allergies will not teach a child to cooperate effectively with a constructive group of kids. Often, though, it really does seem as though treating the disorder has taught a child to read, calculate and cooperate. Curing the disorder makes the child accessible for teaching and training. It permits already learned skills and knowledge to surface. It may enable the child to see and to organize the seeing. The medical disorder is almost always an important part of the character weakness of the disturbing child. Full reeducation is made incredibly difficult without correction of the biological dysfunction.

DIET

Nearly every slum child, most hyperactive and delinquent kids, and many inadequate, weak, *unreactive "tuned-out"* kids habitually do not eat enough proteins—particularly in the morning—and eat too many sweets and simple carbohydrates. Many of these children suffer from hypoglycemia. Any child who persists in troubling or inadequate behavior when a majority of his peers have improved ought to be examined for hypoglycemia. Any internist should be able to run a five hour, seven sample glucose tolerance test and prescribe treatment for the hypoglycemic child. Even if the child does not suffer from hypoglycemia, his diet may create the same functional conditions and improperly fuel both brain and body. Regulation of diet is essential to regulation of behavior.

If the child is in residential care it should be a simple matter to see that sugars, candy, dried fruits, soda and other concentrated sources of sugar are not readily available. Accident rates in factories have been greatly reduced by replacing the soda machine with hot bouillon dispensers. Sugar gives an immediate burst of energy, but rapidly depletes the blood sugar level so that energy and brain functions are drastically reduced. Protein fuels the body in a smoother and longer lasting way. The public schools of Oslo and Pittsburgh now supply children with a high protein supplemental food on arrival at the school—and see that they eat it. The results in improved achievement have been significant.

Food for Millions, P.O. Box 1666, Santa Monica, Calif. 90406, prepares MultiPurpose Food—a completely balanced food, essentially soy grits—which can be baked into cookies, mixed into nearly any other food, or mixed with honey and partially frozen for an attractive and completely nutritious food. Even in day school or outpatient programs it is possible to supplement the diet in a way that gives the child a steady source of energy and ameliorates the effect of the sudden energy losses that are characteristic of a high sugar/carbohydrate diet. Certainly dieticians in residential settings should abolish all processed cereals and breads (noodles, spaghetti, pastries, cakes, Irish potatoes, sugared drinks, candies and dried fruits). Whole grain cereals like Familia or Granola retain the complex structure of the carbohydrates, and breads baked from recently milled whole grains—but no "commercial" breads known to me—also supply a complex carbohydrate that provides a constant supply of energy. It has always amazed me that hospitals and residential treatment centers are willing to spend millions of dollars on needless equipment and superfluous personnel, but can't take the trouble to replace the sponge garbage called bread, the instant potatoes and other overprocessed, depleted "foods" that are the standard diet.

Unfortunately, General Foods and other manufacturers do not make these foods readily available. A good guide book to wholesome natural foods is published by Rodale Press of Emmaus, Pennsylvania.

There really is no simple way out for a conscientious teacher or parent other than hard searching among "health food" stores and other sources. The lackluster, tasteless dietarily correct, but nutritionless mess that is served in the standard public school or hospital cannot be condemned too thoroughly. It is a national disgrace that the wealthiest nation on earth is also one of the most malnourished.

The B complex vitamins include the only enzyme that metabolizes nutrition for the nervous system. Nearly every child sent to us has been found to suffer a deficiency of B vitamins. Whole grains, undebilitated brown rice, eggs, milk and meat from properly fed animals are rapidly disappearing from the market. Consequently the constitutionally less strong individuals are less and less able to maintain adequate nutrition of the nervous system. Hyperactivity and other troubling behavior or inadequacies are always symptoms demanding an inspection both of the B vitamins in the child's ordinary diet, and of his metabolic ability to process the foods. A high intake of sweetened foods will cause a deficiency in the supply of the B complex available to the body and brain. The sugar habits of the child must also be assessed in light of the B vitamin intake.

We have found that C vitamin deficiencies are frequent, but do not seem to be as important as those of the B complex.

Any child who seems suddenly to lose energy in mid-morning or mid-afternoon is likely a victim of poor diet, of a diet unadjusted to his individual ability to process foods, or of hypoglycemia. An alert teacher will note these symptoms and will insist on a full social work report on diet practices in the home, as well as a medical inventory focusing on these factors. If she doesn't have these other professionals available to her, she will determine the facts as best she can on her own. We have never understood the big city trend to isolate teachers from families of their pupils.

Notes on Diet

Diet deprivation may influence several generations even though only one is malnourished (Cowley and Griesel, 1966). The young of rats raised for just one generation on a low protein diet were given a normal diet and did grow better, but when fully grown they were not as good at solving simple problems as normal rats with normal parents. Both growth and development, physical and mental is affected. The rats tend to persist in eating a low protein diet once they are accustomed to it even when an adequate diet is provided. Rats deprived of protein and calories during pregnancy produce young which are smaller, less competent at mazes and more forgetful than their controls (children of the same mother bred to the same father during periods of adequate diet) (Chow, 1966). *New Scientist* (1966) reports two Soviet studies showing that protein deficiency lessens the ability to develop conditional reflexes. They also report that the heavier twin at birth is the brighter, that retarded children tend to be smaller at birth—even if not premature; that children of poorly fed mothers need up to 30 per cent more food to maintain body weight than children of well nourished mothers; that among children whose height is determined by poor diet rather than heredity, the shorter children have lower IQ's and reading ability. Further, dietary deficiencies strike more vigorously at children who, when later given adequate diets, prove to be the stronger, larger, more agile and intelligent.

Toxemia and anoxia, cerebral palsy, epilepsy, mental retardation, behavioral disorganization, and reading disability are functionally related to diet deficiency. Other variables also linked to these problems—race, socioeconomic factors, and weather—are believed to serve primarily as triggers for the dietary trauma (Pasamanick and Knoblock, 1966). Diet deprived people have low thresholds for stress, they are prone to birth casualty, are more likely to have neurological symptoms at birth, and to suffer learning disabilities and behavior disorders. (Knoblock and Pasamanick, 1966). Children severely deprived before six months are likely to lose their intellectual potential; those later deprived usually recover with dietary improvement even though the impairment is severe (Caravioto, 1966). Anan'ev (1966) suggests that the developmental acceleration that has been taking place in all countries in the last 100 years is associated with improvement in nutrition and living conditions.

A high fat diet has an excitatory and beneficial effect on the responses of aging rats in situations putting greater demand on the higher nervous activities (Frankova, 1966). The psychophysical effect of a low protein diet is similar to a state of high physiological arousal—low protein causes a high level of agitated activity. Hyperkinesis is clearly related to dietary deficiencies (Collier, Squibb and Jackson, 1965).

Thiamine deficient rats permitted access to sucrose solution and an iso-caloric corn-oil emulsion for 32 days actually increased their intake of sucrose, and five of seven failed to increase intake of the thiamine-rich corn oil emulsion (Behrman & Maller, 1965). Perseverance of poor diet affecting behavior is a disorder requiring direct and sophisticated intervention. Unfortunately, despite occasional hand-wringing about the poor diets of both poor and affluent kids, nothing substantial is done.

An interesting corollary, the problem of over-nutrition, is shown in two studies of "fasting therapy" with obese patients. No adverse psychological effects were seen after prolonged fasts. There was a slight increase in mental ability, irritability, depression and resistance to testing; but overall self-satisfaction increased strongly. There was somewhat of a reversion to immature, dependent modes of living which did not persist past the fasting period and accelerated behavioral learning. Acquisition and extinction of avoidance responses were facilitated (Murai and Sato, 1965), (Crumpton, Wine and Drenick, 1966).

28

Diet receives some attention in education, but satisfaction with a rather limited concept of "dietician" is too widespread to augur well for the fundamental reexamination that is needed. The Pittsburgh schools discovered malnutrition to be just as high among middle and upper status children as among lower class children and have reproduced the successful "Oslo Breakfast" developed after a similar study in Norway ten years ago. The unfortunate name chosen, "Pittsburgh Yummy Role," hopefully will have no deleterious effect. Both Norway and Pittsburgh reported substantial increase in the general learning curve by providing an early morning nutritional head start (Phi Delta Kappan, 1966).

The reader is further referred to "Malnutrition, Learning, and Behavior," edited by Nevin S. Scrimshow and John E. Gordon, M.I.T. Press, Cambridge, Mass., 1968.

References:

Anan'ev, B. G. Problemy pedagogicheskoi antropologii (Problems of educational anthropology) Sovetskaya Pedagogika, 1966, No. 5, 27-37

Behrman, H. R., & Maller, O. Appetite for sugar and fat in the thiamine deficient rat. Psychonomic Science, 1965, 3(11), 523-524

Caravioto, J. Malnutrition and behavioral development in the pre-school child. Courrier, 1966, 16(2), 117-127

Chow, Bacon. Malnutrition and I.Q. Report in New Scientist, 1966, 33(529), 72

Collier, G. H., Squibb, R. ., & Jackson, F. Activity as a function of diet: I. Spontaneous activity. Psychonomic Science, 1965, 3(5), 173-174

Cowley, J. J. and Griesel, 1966, Animal Behavior, 14(4), 506

Crumpton, E., Wine, D. B., & Drenic, E. J. Starvation: Stress or satisfaction? JAMA, 1966, 196(5), 394-396

Frankova, S. Influence of diet with a different ratio of fat, carbohydrates and protein on the behavior of aging rats. Ceskoslovenska Psychologi, 1966, 10(2), 11-122

Murai, N., & Sato, I. The experimental study of the hunger therapy: I. Effect of starvation upon extinction and acquisition of avoidance response. Tohoku Psychologica Folia, 1965, 24(1-2), 38-45

Pasamanick, B., & Knobloch, H. Retrospective studies on the epidemiology of reproductive casualty: Old and new. Merrill-Palmer Quar., 1966, 12(1), 7-26

Phi Delta Kappan. Nutrition, in Keeping abreast in Education, XLVIII, 4, 183

ALLERGIES

Indigestion, sleepiness, hyperactivity, grogginess or other signs of perceptual inability, as well as a poor or varying attention span, may also be signs of allergic reactions. Most middle class children who have had allergies reacting in the respiratory tract or skin have been evaluated and treated. Unfortunately, the sensitivity of a high portion of the population to foods with allergic reactions not resembling asthma or affecting respiration, has not been as well publicized. Many common foods—peanuts, peanut butter, fish, pork, tomatoes, and eggs are the most common offenders in our experience—cause powerful reactions that affect behavior. Drowsiness, depression, loss of vitality and strength, perceptual debility, and indigestion are frequent results. Often the reduced vitality will lead to excessive activity, loss of control, hostility and other indications of neural disorganization. Many hyperactive children are now routinely treated with amphetamines or other energizers, or are diagnosed as minimal brain injured when actually they are suffering from allergic reactions to common foods. Any child who persists in troubling or inadequate behavior should be tested by a physician, preferably an allergist, for sensitivity to an extensive range of foods and other substances.

The alert teacher can assist the physician by noting behaviors associated with particular foods or environments. If the teacher will note behavior, pulse and respiration rates, perceptual and attention span abilities, both before and after eating, she will be able to point to any large difference in these functions that surely signal allergic reactions.

This paragraph could be included in A THOUSAND AND ONE LESSON PLANS in the appendix, because self study is the most fascinating curriculum of all for children. Teachers who are reading these words and thinking, "Ye gods, does he think the day has 100 hours?" would be well advised to help make children aware of their heart rate, blood pressures, respiration rate, skin response to pressure, to sharp points and to "skin writing" or dermographia. Nothing is more interesting to anyone than himself, and we all, everywhere, say that the function of the school is to help the individual learn who he is. Well, the first thing he is, is a biological entity made of flesh. Man does not live by bread alone, but pure spirit is a very thin diet indeed.

We have seen that many allergies, particularly those resulting in asthma, respond favorably to an improved social setting. Some children never experience another asthma attack after being moved from their home or an inappropriate placement.

It is important that teachers be aware that meals with their children are a very important part of the teaching structure. Most bratty kids have only known meals that were unpleasant—chaotic, poorly prepared and served, noisy, the characteristic time for criticism, punishment and argument. It is important that the adults surrounding the child make the meal relaxed, attractive and pleasant. It is important that programs just before and after meals be pleasant, relaxing and enjoyable. Tests, competitions, commonly detested subject matter (grammar and math) and other anxiety-producing material should certainly be avoided for two hours after meals at the very least.

DEVELOPMENT

Much school failure is due to nothing more than premature demands on children. A middle class child can be taught to read almost instantly at age eight—if he hasn't already taught himself. A bright normal child of four can be taught to read with excitement and care and many hours of work. Why do it? By the age of twelve it will make little difference if the child learned to read at four or eight, all other things being equal.

There is absolutely no evidence that school ability has any relationship to *adult success,* anyway, except at the gross lower end. Many children have escaped school until age twelve or older, and, as long as their parents were verbal and competent at various skills, they have caught up in a year or less. As of 1970 there is absolutely no evidence that any particular school experience is more helpful than any other for children.

In our experience nearly all the children sent to us for serious behavior problems or school failures are developmentally behind their age norm (the Gesell people have reported on some school districts in which *more than* half the kids are behind the "norm"). While it is true that most kids do not fit the ideal developmental scheme, it is also true that *all* children, as they grow older, find it easier to accomplish complex tasks, abstracting tasks, tasks requiring attention and refinement, tasks requiring mental or physical dexterity, and tasks requiring discrimination. If a child were absolutely isolated from complicating experiences he would lose most of his abilities. It is a ridiculous anxiety even for slum parents to think that their kids won't learn; it is a totally absurd anxiety for middle class parents. Slums may be more complex environments than suburbs but it is absurd to think that kids freely living in either will not learn. Unfortunately, the absurdity doesn't prevent it from having currency. One wonders what kind of reasoning can justify buying all kinds of materials for "perceptual enrichment" for kids who live in the most complex, artifact-filled environment ever known. And kids who are taken for a run through woods, creeping, crawling, jumping, dodging, will be training their perceptual abilities through means infinitely more complex than a training kit in a classroom.

Most children in trouble need time to catch up their growth—physical, emotional and cognitive. Nearly all childish problem behaviors disappear by age twenty-five, including some pretty difficult problems like heroin addiction and many instances of mental retardation and homosexuality. An apparently irreducible percentage of difficult characters remain—criminal, psychotic, neurotic, failing and addicted. There is no evidence that anyone knows what to do with these characters.

There is very good evidence that reducing the pressures on childish and adolescent offenders reduces the incidence of their failures. For example, kids who drop out of school are *arrested* more often while they are in school. Dropouts do *not* commit more crimes than kids who remain in school. There are more juvenile crimes committed on school nights than on weekends and holidays. The evidence indicates that the successful middle class child who also commits crimes carries out much more destructive and serious offenses than dropouts and lower class offenders.

The one American ethnic group that produces almost no delinquency confounds the usual assumptions about the causes of delinquency. The American Chinese are likely one of the most indulgent groups of parents in America. Their children are not weaned until after age two. Bedtimes for school age children *begin* around 8:30 and very young children can be seen out on the streets at 10 or later. Nearly every expression of childish enjoyment is supported and nurtured except violence and aggression. The orderliness and gentleness of these children by the time they reach school age is phenomenal. It is quite likely that for this reason they experience school in a much different way than do other Americans who are raised in a concept of childhood that supposes child care should be like Army Basic Training—preparation for war. Indulgence is the one thing a teacher need not be afraid to offer.

Most treatment centers report large numbers of children whose failures or troubling behavior completely disappear almost immediately after transfer to the center. It is very clear that inappropriate demands on the child can create substantial difficulties. If the reader doubts this, try the simple experiment of signing your name while swinging in a clock-wise motion, the foot which corresponds to your writing hand. Children forced to perform beyond their developed capacity experience the same sense of impossibility and frustration you will feel if you persist at this "task." Imagine carrying out such tasks all day long! Kids are made to.

A good teacher has to remember that skills almost impossible to teach at one age are easily taught at another. No child is without skills. The effective teacher will focus on existing skills to find the level of development at which the child now works. By complicating and enlarging the existing skills the good teacher avoids not only premature pressure on the child but also the trap of infantilizing the child and boring him by asking him to do too little. Every organism is born with a posture of growth and expansion toward the future. It is critical that the child's optimistic posture of growth toward the future be cherished and sustained. This posture is destroyed both by demands beyond his competence, and by abandoning the child to less than appropriate demands. The important principle is that the *child* ought to be the source of data and guidance.

Various books by Ames and Ilg give detailed and useful guidance about development to teachers. While the Gesell people are criticized by some theorizers, they are among the very few professionals who work with large numbers of children and who publish extensive and detailed data accessible for criticism, replication or refutation. An enormous amount of busy work, particularly in "perceptual training" and "remedial reading" is simply unnecessary, and often teaches the child an inflexible pattern of failure by boring him to tears.

Nearly everyone has heard something about the Freudian concepts of psychosexual development, concepts which serve little or no practical purpose. It is interesting that almost no one, including most psychologists, knows that the way children learn evolves through ages and levels of development. Emotional responses are the most important kind of learning. Emotion learned even before birth affects much of subsequent behavior. Emotional responses, learned through spinal reflex conditioning, or "Pavlovian conditioning," is almost the only form of learning available to the infant (it is also called classical conditioning, emotional conditioning or Type S conditioning). Spinal reflex conditioning mainly develops emotional reactions. This is the basic type of conditioning needed if one wants to set up emotional responses or to train in motivation.

I suppose I should apologize to my poor reader at this point for throwing in a lot of technical Choctaw, especially having promised not to talk about the theoretic underpinning of the techniques in this HANDBOOK. However, it is critically important that parents and teachers remember that the first mode of learning is by paired associations—Mama's warm body equals yummy milk; smiling face equals tickle and cuddle; nice smell equals calm Mommy, etc., etc. It is also critically important for parents to remember that under pressure of any kind kids regress; they slip back to the earlier kinds of learning. The child that is tired, hungry, bored, frustrated, frightened, anxious or otherwise under pressure may slip back to spinal reflex conditioning in which the only way he can learn is by· paired associations. This is also the most powerful form of learning, that persists longest and disappears last. Almost all the basic skills— walking, talking, seeing, hearing, reading, are established by this kind of learning. A lot of reading difficulty occurs because teachers overcomplicate the matter and think that it has something to do with reason. Reading is no more complex a skill than walking or hearing and is primarily a primitive skill, despite the fact that it appears late in human history.

Of course, brain damaged children, children with severe emotional disorders, or retarded children can frequently be taught only by paired associations, using pleasurable experiences and associations already established to enlarge the range of behavior and knowledge. It is perverse, of course, not to try at least, this kind of teaching when other kinds don't seem to work.

By one year the baby starts actively to deal with its environment with its body. During this period spinal reflex conditioning becomes less important and a kind of learning called *peripheral* conditioning becomes the main learning process. This is also called motor learning, precision learning, response shaping, instrumental conditioning, Type "R" conditioning and operant conditioning. This type of learning increases the precision and effectiveness with which the child uses his muscles to manipulate or modify his environment. Peripheral conditioning uses higher neural centers than spinal reflex conditioning, and under stress the simpler form of learning, emotion, comes to the fore and affects all subsequent learning.

From eighteen months to about age four or five verbal learning emerges. Verbal learning initially is very direct and does not importantly involve problem solving. The child learns descriptions, directions, and can code memories verbally. This type of learning is characterized by very rapid coding, single presentations of vivid material being all that is necessary in most cases. It is interesting to note that "don't" and "no" appear in all cultures and language groups before "do" and "yes." The first person singular, "I," also appears late in all groups. This is important to remember when assessing the interaction between the first kinds of learning and verbal learning. Many difficulties are related to the fact that there is no smooth interaction between emotional/motor learning (spinal/reflex peripheral nerves learning) and verbal learning (learning in the cortex).

I have been this technical only because I believe it to be absolutely essential for parents and teachers to remember clearly the increasing sophistication of learning modes, and the fact that children, and adults, slip back to earlier modes under pressure. Remembering that paired association (spinal reflex) learning precedes learning by reward and punishment, that the child can hear and understand and follow commands before giving them, that he will give commands before he can transact or communicate in a give and take kind of way, is also useful and will help parents and teachers avoid difficulty in teaching.

Spinal Reflex
Motor Reflex
Verbal Input (Receiving Commands)
Verbal Output (Giving Commands)
Communication/Conversation/Transaction
Intuition/Gestalt/Creativity

This is a very oversimplified outline of the means by which people learn. It is important for parents and teachers to remember this organization because the more sophisticated, mature, *later* forms of learning crumple under pressure and disappear. Just as the child will act much younger when he is hungry or frustrated, he will learn in a much younger mode when he is frustrated or anxious. All these kinds of learning go on all the time as well, and some bad learning that has occurred by one means will not be unlearned through another means. That is, all the talking in the world will almost never "cure" a phobia, the habit of wetting the bed, etc.; while very simple techniques discussed below will almost immediately "cure" phobias and bedwetting.

At the age in which the verbal system is strongly emerging (2-3) children cannot switch verbally induced behaviors. For example, tell a child to put a ring on a dowel; once he starts the action he cannot stop nor can he put the ring on another dowel. He will intensify the *first* requested action if he is asked to stop or switch. Inducements will only increase the intensification of the first request. Conflict, ambiguity, and trauma during this period can set up a permanent style of behavior reflecting the early emergency of "no" and "don't" and the amplifying effects of contradictory and negative commands. It is very important to remember that under hunger, boredom, stress, fatigue or frustration the child regresses to an earlier stage, and may become fixed there.

By four or five years most children are beginning to learn at a verbal reasoning or cognitive level (cognitive strategies appear even in the lowest animals and in children at a preverbal level). This learning permeates the cortex of the brain, and uses the highest level of nervous organization. This kind of learning has also been called insight learning and Gestalt (Ah-Ha!) learning. Cognitive learning involves a reorganization of labelled events associated with other memories into new structures arranged in ways which make sense to the child. The relevance of the associations enables the child to understand the material in his remembered matrix of frameworks and actively to organize new experiences.

Remembering the stages of the growth of learning may be of use to teachers in two ways. It may allow the teacher to choose a training method or program best suited to the goals sought in the classroom (e.g., spinal reflex conditioning for training emotions or motivations; peripheral conditioning for training motor or cognitive or perceptual precision; vivid presentation with motor/verbal interaction for learning new words, skills like reading and basic arithmetic; and cognitive training for reorganization of events to make sense for the child). It may also allow the teacher to use other means to train when the child is relatively unable to learn by a standard method (e.g., a child might not be able to learn effectively by means of insights given him in verbally presented material, say, because the child has cortical brain damage, but he may still be able to learn by repeatedly pairing a new symbol or experience with one known to evoke a desired response in the child, that is, by spinal reflex conditioning).

SLEEP

We have been increasingly impressed by the importance of sleep to behavior. It is well known that prisons and mental hospitals have a difficult time during the full moon. We suspect that this mystery is due to nothing more than the fact that excessive light, and very normal biological rhythms, disrupt regular sleep—particularly in weaker organisms. After years of experimenting with allowing children to establish their own sleep patterns, we are now committed to firm management of sleep times. In residential settings any change in the sleep cycle is an effective predictor of outbreaks of troubling behavior. If a residential program can afford the physical and staff structure, a great deal of difficulty will be eliminated by separating individuals who spontaneously arise early in the morning from the night people—both staff and students or inmates. Unfortunately, most cannot afford this structure; but, it is an amazingly powerful tool for increasing work capacity and reducing conflict and aberration.

Frequently "night people" are anxiety responders. That is they respond to events with sympathetic nervous system activity, or anxiety. By evening their level of anxiety is very high and sleep is difficult if not impossible. Relaxation procedures, strenuous physical exercise or awareness-building procedures—all described below—will aid in regulating this problem.

Difficult kids often seem sleepy a good deal of the time. They may be reported to have "sleepy eyes," fogged out attention, and hyperactivity. When the same individual also resists sleeping while seeming to be on the verge of sleep a good deal of the time, and once having fallen asleep is very difficult to awaken, we can be certain that effective sleep regulation will improve behavior.

Most so-called psychopaths and character-disordered children will live in this pattern. If dietary factors, hypoglycemia and allergies are ruled out by a physician, these children can be regarded as "functional narcoleptics."

We call this pattern the Henry Chicken Hawk syndrome (after the old cartoon series). Henry, a chicken hawk chick complete with rucked-up hair, sleepy eyes and defiant face, never seemed to learn that he couldn't beat up big roosters, steal eggs or chickens bigger than he. Disaster after disaster, punishment after punishment, scolding after scolding had no effect. Old sleepy eyes would rush off again for the next immediate thrill. Whoever wrote the series must have known, or been, a delinquent brat.

Functional narcolepsy can be carefully diagnosed by a neurologist by presenting mildly bothersome statements to an unsedated child while running an electroencephalogram. If sleep spindles of 12 and 14 cycle per second spikes appear, then narcolepsy is indicated. During the disarmoring presentations discussed below, if the student falls asleep during the routine and is a "Henry Chicken Hawk," narcolepsy is probably his problem. Any individual who habitually responds to stress with signs of sleep should have a good neurological work-up. A rapid burst of eyeblinks while talking, particularly talking about something that exposes the self, while lying, or defending, or other stressful talking will also be a good indicator—particularly if it is the habitual style of the individual. In fact, excessive blinking, by itself, is a fairly reliable indicator of narcolepsy.

Under supervision of a physician, this pattern may be regulated by prescription of a psychic energizer (amphetamine, imipramine-like compounds, or monoamine oxidase inhibitors, Dexedrine,

Ritalin, or Deaner). Rigid management of bedtime and bedtime environment, and other regulating tactics will also assist. It is important to know that the failure of one drug does not indicate the absence of narcolepsy. Ritalin will often work where Dexedrine will not—and sometimes the system is so powerful that very large doses over a long period of time are indicated. A physician will be able to regulate the dosage correctly with the assistance of good observation from the teacher.

Both narcolepts and students who do not show as strong a narcoleptic pattern, but whose sleep patterns are askew (usually late night prowling, partial insomnia, etc., rather then early morning inability to sleep or frank insomnia) can be regulated by initiating a sequence of a forty-eight or seventy-two hour wake marathon ended at about the regular bedtime. Very disturbed schizophrenics will establish a basic sleep cycle after one seventy-two hour wake marathon followed by a period of sedated sleep (preferably using a mixture of soporiphic compounds) followed by a seventy-two hour marathon and a period of unsedated sleep. However, orderly behavior can also be established in psychotic patients by regularizing sleep through a compound hypnotic drug. These pharmaceutical tactics, of course, are available only under medical supervision; however, the teacher should be alert for signs of sleep cycle disturbance to report to the physician.

Marathon wake sessions without drugs often satisfactorily regulate sleep. They also rapidly establish rapport in a new group, and may wear out anti-social habits. It does not seem important what kind of activities are used to keep the group awake so long as they are not overtly destructive.

In cases of frank insomnia, where the student reports discomfort and a wish to regularize sleep, a daily session in which he is instructed to try to stay awake, preferably doing something mildly unpleasant like scrubbing a floor, or simply sitting up—but not reading or in bed—will rapidly end the problem. The instruction ought to be given forcefully and repeatedly.

Teachers will seldom see a frankly insomniac adolescent or child. Kids in my experience prize their sleep irregularities and will struggle to maintain them. Once in a great while a bright brat will catch onto the fact that the teacher sees sleep regulation as very important, and, instead of negatively reacting in the usual Tom Sawyer way, will make the insomniac game of "I really want to sleep, and I'm so unhappy I can't" his major tool for teacher manipulation. In almost every case the brat will avoid taking his drug prescription, push hard and sneakily at bedtime boundaries, fog out at every opportunity, and in every possible way, except verbally, demonstrate that he has learned to use sleep resistance as his way of handling anxiety. The waking/sleep process is a very useful tool for the brat, and is the primary reason these kids never learn from punishment or consequences in reality. They simply aren't around.

THE ECOLOGY OF BEHAVIOR

While most ecological issues are beyond the control of the average teacher these introductory comments would be incomplete without mention of the incredible importance of physical structures, size, shape, color, texture, mass, attitude, position, and relationships to behavior. Temperature, ambient noise and airflow, sources and qualities of light, often control gross behavior, organic physical development, and the important emotional and motivational states of the person.

Probably the least healthy environment for children ever devised was the "railroad" tenement. The loss of privacy, the driving of noise and constant contact with others, the sense of vulnerability and ease of abrasion with each other is duplicated only in barracks, hospital wards and schools. It is interesting to note that rats, usually good family animals, become thoroughly depraved with complete social and family collapse in only three generations of removal from separate private nesting environments into tenement nesting arrangements in which each nest opens into the other.

Privacy and safety are critical for learning of all kinds. It is certain that the highly anxious, frightened child who is the typical failure or troublemaker needs more rather than less privacy, more rather than less safety and insulation. It is essential that structures be created in the classroom, if they are but large cardboard cartons and paper block walls, that enable children to build safety and privacy into their social life at school.

It is, of course, important that the school room be attractive to the pupil. This seldom means the nice orderly displays that so delight a certain type of pedagogue. Children love bright, vivid, dynamically ordered relationships and structures. A classroom that does not reflect this electricity is a classroom that actively harms children. The schoolroom can be in a gloomy and ancient building, but have vitality built into it by a good teacher working with her children.

The British and Scandinavians have enjoyed a great deal of success with junk playgrounds (now, for obvious reasons, renamed "adventure" playgrounds). In these playgrounds a fenced-off lot or field is piled high with old lumber and other building materials. A shack is erected for the only adult present—a facilitator—who sees that tools are handed out, with nails and other small goods. He prevents the worst mayhem, and helps out as asked. He is not a program director or supervisor. It is fascinating how these junk playgrounds go through, each summer, an identical cycle. First there is private hoarding and hiding, the building of independent and isolated caves for robbers and pirates, with a great deal of suspicion. Next, small gangs of robbers and such will form, eventually growing into fully organized communities with hospitals, schools, jails, apartments and the like. It is as if the kids recreate cooperative society each year, unlearning the antisocial viciousness they are taught in the home, church and school and living out the hatefulness that has been distilling for nine long months. Only one of the many measures of success of the junk playgrounds is the fact that their insurance rates are now lower than those of standard playgrounds.

If the teacher does not have such richly complex structures

available to her it is possible to enlarge the social field of the class in other ways. In ten years of taking children caving, mountain climbing, wilderness camping, survival camping, canoeing, city rambling, car tours, camping out overnight with only sleeping bags and cold lunches, and island hopping, we have never suffered a serious accident. The teacher who cannot provide some of these experiences for her students even without the financial support of the school can hardly be considered a serious teacher. The residential school that does not include these activities as a normal and integral part of its program can hardly be regarded as even ethical.

There are many means of enriching the social structure of the standard classroom—even when the school administration is restrictive. A simple way of enriching the ecology is to break the age segregation. Kids teaching kids is the most effective social and teaching model now reported in the literature. If this is prohibited by the administration, then using better students to teach the worse, enlarging the social responsibility of students, forming separate work, play and study teams, and creating focus areas in the classroom will enlarge the choice available to kids. It will enable them more rapidly to find their own level of work and progress away from it.

An ideal elementary classroom has at least two teachers, and often involves as many as ten at one time (by teachers of course I mean volunteers, aides and "real" teachers—all used to advance the transactions of learning and not just for janitorial, nursing and secretarial tasks). The number of students can be more than thirty or so. The room should be large and ideally has an easily accessible half-second-story for reading and solitary quiet study or withdrawal for sleep or sloth. ("Il dolce fariente"—sweet do nothing, is really *useful* in the class.) The main room is organized with formal foci—messy corners, neat book corners, production corners and display corners. A separated or semi-separated area for noisy, messy, destructive and constructive shop work, biology or what have you is also ideal. A less than ideal classroom can be a single small room with too many children and no partitions or semi-partitions, and still be organized into foci of activities, emotional styles, activity rhythms, and momentary-emotional-identity-of-the-child.

I have worked with two other teachers in an absolutely bare room, 40 x 50 feet, with 100 illiterate, preschool children of migrant farmers and have been satisfied that our accomplishment was more than if we had separated into three classes. The two core teachers establish themselves as activity and emotional poles in the room. A single teacher can use the physical arrangement of furniture, rugs, railings, cardboard boxes, chalk lines on the floor or quite imaginary force fields and boundaries to establish the same ecological distribution. Of course it is easier with actual raised floors, semi-partitions, room dividers, shelves, etc. Lack of equipment, however, is never an excuse for less structure, but a command and imperative for more, richer, more fluid and dynamic structure. Unfortunately, most people think the word "structure" is limited to something like the military hierarchy and the pseudo-structure of the lecture room and textbook. It is as if biologists thought that a crystal or even a block of homogenous and undifferentiated matter had more structure than a living cell.

Without directing the children to either pole, the teachers move into scheduled activity as the day begins. One pole is active, out-going, louder—attending to painting, clay, building, rambling outside, beginning reading. The other is quieter and more passive—story reading, writing, building songs and other less noisy activity. It is important that these divisions not be fixed in merely mechanistic fashion; any teacher may perform any task in the school room. Every effort should be made to associate books, schooling, reading with a relaxed purposiveness.

It is also important to see that such a classroom can be organized without the presence of a teacher. The main reason we have to have teachers is that our kids have violently been taught that order and production depend on the presence of adults—COPS. However, we are able to create a classroom on a slum corner without the copping presence of a police-teacher by introducing vivid materials attended by a peer or near-peer. When we have as many as a third of a class who have been with us before, we are able simply to turn on the machine—the ecologically sound classroom—and leave it operating all day with minimum adult involvement. It should be perfectly obvious that you can't do this in the common classroom because the common classroom is a machine designed for easy training of animals into domesticated consumers. The common class machine has got to have a domesticator. You can populate a quite bare room and, having built a society of leaders supported by a democratically active citizenry, leave them quite productively—as long as you don't depart with "I trust you to behave." This means, of course, "I DON'T TRUST YOU."

You can start by selecting the five socially most competent kids, (invariably including at least one of your worst problems), and engaging them in the teaching vocation. Kids understand very readily that the ordinary school has got to have quiet and order—even if only because the principal is a jerk. They are vitally interested in helping you succeed in the jungle war needed to make their day vital, creative, productive and fun. If quiet is a price, they'll cheerfully pay it.

These five kids can be assigned to five groups of six, or to areas of the room as managers of specific skills and activities. Others can have the function of signalling that the noise/behavior level has passed the threshold—by turning off the lights (signal for absolute quiet), sounding a signal, turning on special lights, etc. Others can plan actions. (How close do they come to an "Educational" experience on one of those useless tours they usually drowse through?) They will push for excitement, food, deviltry, adventure; you will push for something that can be displayed as quiet, orderly, neat and safe. Objectify the conflict and talk about it. Why shouldn't the subject of the class, even the youngest class, or the quite retarded, be *itself?* Why not admit the rituals and taboos of the society in which it must daily move? The important thing is that in the content of the subject, and the styles, tempos and locations in which it is studied, the teacher ought to be doing things about the structure of the learning ecology. She has the job of enriching, complicating and making it more reasonable, natural, organic and powerful.

The richer the selection of artifacts, gadgets, objects, spaces and relationships, the busier, more purposive and satisfactory the behavvior of the pupils is going to be. This is particularly so if the artifacts are simple, vivid, and uncluttered, with classic, dramatic lines and bare faces. It will be even more so if the possibilities of the environment allow the artifacts, gadgets, objects, spaces and relationships to be taken apart as well as put together.

Within the framework of such principles, nearly any accommodation can be made with the social realities of the limitations required by the psychoses of the school administration. It is simply a question of the teacher getting to be on the side of the kids. Then, they can help her. Until that time, it's just a wrestling match no matter how skillfully done.

THE TOM SAWYER EFFECT

Many of us usually react in a generally negative way to instructions, commands, social demands and cooperative needs or admonitions that we seem to recognize readily. Apparently this recognition is clear for the negativism is oriented against the positive input. It has been observed that delinquents and criminals seem more, rather than less, moralistic and authoritarian in their verbal values than the general population. They are not "moral imbeciles," at least not in their intellectual awareness of right and wrong.

I am not talking about the kids who reject the Vietnam war and perform various negative acts in opposition or deliberately become incompetent to avoid the draft. All of the people I am talking about are negative toward things they say they respect. They are incompetent in ways that are not apparently deliberate, but self-defeating if their own statements about themselves are serious. Of course some are so far gone that they make no statements about what they think about themselves. But, at the very least, they usually look unhappy.

Would it be useful to use a broad, common sense grouping similar to this for talking about a general program of re-education? These descriptions seem to include most criminals, delinquents, management problems, underachievers, neurotics, psychotics, socially maladjusted, learning problems, and people who fail the "mental" tests for the draft, etc. Particularly by identifying two groups of "nay sayers," we can include nearly every behavior problem and avoid medical, psychic and moral categories. These are: 1) people who seek conflict with authority and seem to be seeking punishment or intense sensations, and 2) people who effectively avoid authority but are characteristically ineffective at other self-serving goals.

Despite the broad generality of these descriptions, they do seem to provide a framework for understanding some difficulties that occur when current theories about learning are exposed to fairly common behavior:

1. Children who are immediately okay when removed from home and put in a supportive environment.

2. Illiterate children who quickly teach themselves to read in a new environment.

3. The fact that ten or twelve effective techniques can be used to instill a behavior desired by an authority, any one of which contradicts a theory on which the other is based, e.g., a child who constantly gets out of his chair in class can be persuaded or compelled or induced or otherwise caused to sit in the chair during the prescribed times by:

a. talking to him, particularly if a powerful peer or a new and liked authority does the talking;

b. ignoring his leaving the chair;

c. rewarding his leaving the chair;

d. repeatedly punishing his leaving the chair;

e. using a single symbolic punishment of his leaving the chair;

f. responding to his leaving the chair with a different behavior each time (either an expectable behavior or a bizarre behavior);

g. responding to the child on a random schedule with either a repeated or different behavior;

h. ordering the child to leave the chair;

i. punishing him for staying in the chair.

4. The fact that most of these people stop this kind of behavior (including surprising groups like drug addicts) by the time they are 25 and are left only with social and educational liabilities which are not too noticeable, may only be formal; they are both spontaneously and programmatically remediable.

5. Nonverbal autistics choose objects they are instructed to pick out of a tray at significantly less than chance level.

6. Test scores can be effectively predicted by a suggestibility measure, indicating that test ability in an instruction situation may reflect nothing more than a person's reaction to instruction *per se*.

7. Dropouts commit more crimes while they are in school than after dropping out, and there are more crimes by kids on school days than on weekends and holidays.

8. The well known self-destructiveness and guilt in criminals, alcoholics and junkies, always very well verbalized and to some extent repeated in the behavior and talk of neurotics and psychotics, as well as psychopaths.

9. The persistent two-thirds success rate of psychotherapies which remains persistently just under the persistent rate of spontaneous recovery.

10. The persistent success of Summerhill-type schools, organic teaching methods, teaching by peers, recovery of school skills by the dropouts to about the average of their social class, and the success of democratically reorganized mental hospital wards and out-patient clinics.

11. The persistence of negative behavior in the face of experience, instruction, knowledge, belief, punishment and stated desires.

It may be that these behaviors can all be seen as intensities of responses based on a disorder in talking behavior. If a two year old is asked to put a ring on a spindle and then, as the child complies, told "no, put it on the other one," the child cannot change. The first action will be intensified even if strong incentives are offered for changing. This is about the age that the "don't put jam on the cat" phenomenon first appears. Any child worker can show how children can be made to do exactly what they are told not to do and will stop doing what they are told to do. This appears cyclically in small children, is incredibly strong at some stages and persists in every hyperactive, unmanageable child that we have seen or read about. Could we deal with these people on a basis of understanding them as linguistically disordered within a matrix of genetic and constitutional factors that also effect behavior?

Professionals have often worked with children who are physical paragons and psychopathic in the extreme, physically deviant only in the tension of their muscles and their facial expressions. All of us have seen children with serious physical liabilities who are paragons of resourcefulness, courage, cooperation and skill. Every social population produces individuals at the poles of competence and only severe disorders like Mongolism produce populations with no effective individuals. This fact always poses serious difficulties for every theory of causes.

We have found over 87 per cent of our children to be suffering from nutritional deficiency, over 80 per cent from an allergy strongly affecting perception and vitality, and over 80 per cent from some other defect. However, the Peckham Health Centre found 86 per cent of men and 97 per cent of women in a normal population suffering from some disease giving at least moderate disability and discomfort. The old dichotomies are not useful in any effective theory or treatment. It ought to be simple to devise value scales for allergies, enzyme imbalances, deficiencies and diseases, as well as kinetic abilities and general constitutional strength and flexibility, and thus be able to weigh predictions for the rapidity of social and intellectual re-education. It is certainly clear that a whole host of behaviors are learned and even if a condition like early infantile autism is constitutional, a physical cure is not going to leave the individual with intact social and intellectual skills. The fact that some autistic children have made complete reversals in very brief periods creates difficulty for some theories, but underlines the fact that linguistic disturbance may be established by one-trial traumatic learning and reversed by a similar process.

Traumatic neuroses seem to be set up when a traumatic event occurs without warning and is accompanied by strong painful sensations (embarrassment may be understood as painful in this sense). When there is no time for avoiding the event because of little, or no, or unclear warning, the result often is immobility, or movement experiences as irrelevant or impotent. One-trial learning, particularly of automobile phobias or neuroses, can easily be demonstrated this way.

Other powerful reactions, also occuring this way, are self-reinforcing. A cycle of memory and intensification of subsequent similar experiences does not readily disappear. For example, we ask a subject to stop for a moment and think of personal experiences in school, and then to think quickly of the first time he was greatly embarrassed in school. Nearly everyone remembers an event that occurred suddenly, was acutely embarrassing and about which nothing could be done. Most of the average person's difficulty with authority and lack of ease in social situations requiring good control or display, comes through the multiplication of such events. Think of the average mother's technique of spit-bathing children, witness the agitation and impotence that accompanies it, and you will see how dirt neuroses and fixations could occur.

It seems reasonable to suggest that sometime during the period in which talking is first coming fluent in children, such one-trial learning experiences occur in a way that locks the verbal system into a negative coding of instructions. This coding would be even more distorted when perceptual and motor or constitutional weaknesses are present. Once the verbal system is fully developed it would seem that similar one-trial learning experiences are primarily dealt with by physical reactions: allergies, cancer, heart and digestive diseases.

It has been shown that people emerging from long periods of compressed rage or other strong emotional states develop moderate to strong food allergies which duplicate some of the rage sensations.

Physical deficiencies may well account for the intensity and general direction of disorders in the verbal system and their consequences in behavior. However, most of this learning usually comes in response to an authority, an external power or a social matrix that controls and shapes behavior. It is not too difficult to see the equivalence of nearly all embarrassments, experiences of impotence, extreme discomfort, enforced immobility and other experiences sufficiently strong to condition single trial learning, whether they are commands, instructions and restraints, or pains, embarrassments and terrors. They are authoritative structures—externally controlling events. It doesn't really matter if they are presented to the child in a "loving" or in a "hateful" way. The linguistic coding takes place in either event. This is probably why children of disciplinarian, but consistent, parents are seldom delinquent. Since consistently permissive parents also seldom produce delinquent children, the reliability (consistency) of the external coding seems to be what is important.

Consider that traumatic conditioning occurs only after a sequence of events in a particular order, together with the fact that it is deconditionable by subsequent experience; notice that physical variables can strongly modify such learning; then you can see why only some children learn a habitually negative way of responding. In fact, it probably demands a high level of skill and persistence on the part of the adults around the child to crank in this unnatural response. However, simple experiments with any conversation will readily demonstrate that nearly everyone has habitual responses to strong commands and definite statements of fact. The "don't put jam on the cat" syndrome is not merely a childish phenomenon.

The little child experiences this universal dissonance merely as a playful exercise of his new power to organize the world verbally. It is only when it becomes his chief means of successfully avoiding pain caused by adults and "instructions" that it becomes a style of life.

II
PSYCHOKINETICS

TENDER LOVING CARE

In our society it is easier and socially more acceptable to express anger, hostility, rejection, aloofness, and criticism than affection, warmth, desire, approval or satisfaction. The tides of love have been at ebb flood for a long time and only recently, in superficial ways, do we see any evidence of change.

We have been impressed by the almost total inability of troubling adolescents to express or accept positive emotions. We have been amazed to see how seldom such children touch themselves or others, at how little physical flexibility even the best of them have, at how limited is their ability at nonverbal kinetic communication, how poor their mimetic ability, and how congested their emotions. We are often sent children with histories indicating many rage experiences. We never see this behavior more than once or twice at our centers (probably because we simply restrain and ignore it in a very blunt and matter of fact way) and the few initiating times we do see it, it appears to us much more as display and histrionics than emotional expression.

Children need to be touched. Infants cannot go about their biological task of differentiating nerve endings, sophisticating perceptions and movements, without the assistance of a great deal of touching by others. In the families of most failing and difficult children, touching is limited to bare essentials, and to punishment erratically and unjustly exploded out of adult needs. Animals deprived of touching and contact with other animals are in many ways less healthy, smaller, less capable. Animals held and fondled by human experimenters are more competent than those which are not.

Hold a new born foal in your arms until it calms, several days in a row. After it begins to walk, coax it to you with gentle sounds and apples or sugar, pet it until it gentles. Go away for a year. Come back and for several days coax the colt to you again, put your arms around it, pet it until it gentles. The entire "personality" of the horse will change. It will be more adventurous than other colts, leaving its mother to explore. It will be resourceful in emergencies— it won't panic in a fire, it will be more alert to danger in general. If someone tries to cross a road when a car is coming, such a horse has been known to stop a person. If it gets its head caught in a fence it will, unlike other horses, not fruitlessly pull and pull until exhausted and hurt beyond recovery. It will calmly remove its head. The total time of intervention thoroughly to change the "natural" personality of the horse is about an hour a day for two weeks, separated by a year. An "autistic" animal becomes an open, expressive, adventuring and reliable animal simply as a result of brief infantile training. Even the sounds the horse makes will be unusual!

We believe that touching is so important that we actually run a "love-up" rota of staff in our elementary residential programs. Even the most wooden staff member is received with delight. Each child is tickled, rubbed, fondled, patted and kissed goodnight with special words of affection and joy. I am always impressed at the willingness of otherwise tough and aloof teenage criminals to accept this "baby" treatment. Our experience is sufficiently convincing that we persist in touching those teenagers who strongly reject touching. The weaker staff is not encouraged to take on these kids but strong staff members will tease and ridicule the aloofness and pursue and persist in touching.

While some assaultive boy/girl touching may go on in a pseudo-sexual way—particularly if they think that an adult is going to be offended by the activity—most troubling youngsters cannot and will not readily, gently or communicatively touch others. Quite the contrary. Investigations of promiscuous girls have revealed that the "sexual" behavior is almost always as untouching as possible. It is, of course, not really sexual or even pleasurable behavior, but behavior directed at self-degradation and power. This inhibition is particularly true of homosexuals and prostitutes.

TOUCHING GAMES

Increasing the enjoyment of other people is one of the most effective means of recreating socially constructive behavior in troubling youngsters. From earliest kindergarten through adult programs we have enjoyed a great deal of success by institutionalizing, ritualizing and programming increasing physical contact with self and others.

A self-conscious routine is always less useful than one which can be forced by the structure of the environment or procedure. For example, an obstacle course that requires mutual assistance to traverse is better than a routine that directs holding or touching; for the same kind of reasons, caving, hill climbing where there are many sharp gullies and fallen trees, and other events in the field are better than obstacle courses. In general we try to use strenuous and complex activities in as complex a field situation as possible. Where such program is not practicable we evolve exercises based on the same principles.

OBSTACLE COURSES

CONFIDENCE COURSES—These courses are gentler than obstacle courses and are designed to build and demonstrate confidence. Pit jumps, rope swings, incline balances, level beams six feet in the air, ladder climbs of varying difficulty, rope slides and other semi-barriers are built into courses of varying difficulty.

BEACH AND POOL—Water games, chicken fights and other horseplay ordinarily prohibited in swimming programs are natural and useful. The program, of course, is designed for the environment. Tag games perfectly safe at the beach are dangerous around a pool. Horseplay in a large pool with active and alert staff engaged in the play is as safe as any other sport. Drownproofing and other formal courses of instruction where the individual compares himself to his own past ability are excellent.

INDOOR ROUTINES—Indoor games are infinite in number: choosing teams and passing an orange or ball while hands remain behind backs, using only the grasp of chin against neck; lodging a cube held on a small paddle in a basket or bag attached to the back of your opponent's belt while he tries to put his cube in your basket (both standing with feet still); transferring a marble from spoons held in team members' mouths in a race against another team—the list is inexhaustible.

Often just having the class sit, crawl, lie or otherwise arrange themselves in a novel way is quite productive.

Sit the group in a circle with feet extended. Draw up left knees and hug the knee tightly. Then rub the knee and let loose all over. Do the same for the other knee. Do the same all over the body—both hands. Have the class talk to their knees as if they were persons, boy or girl friends; "ham" it up.

While sitting in a circle have the class pair off. Each one is to reach out and touch the other one. Then tell them to touch the other somewhere else. Then tell them to touch the other on the face. Tell the one on the right to tell the other what he sees as he touches the other. Reverse.

Have the group lift up one person. Lower and lift again. Have a blanket toss. Congo line. While doing other exercises suddenly tell the group—"Everyone hug someone else," make them continue and be vigorous about it. Switch to require boy/girl, or same sex.

Play blind man's bluff, blind man identify. Play all blind and find your partner without talking: grunting and other noises allowed.

While seated, play follow the leader for movements, facial gestures, noises, etc., but no talking except shouted slogans, emotional outbursts, etc.

Have a group move large, but not too heavy artifacts—poles, constructs, etc., that require many helpers. Build a special obstacle hall to encourage awkward positions and other problems.

Have groups sit in small circles and instruct them to "see how long you can keep silent. You may talk, but if you do, see if you can talk about why you are talking, and see if the group can stay quiet again."

Pair off for exercises (see below) that require help.

Pair off for back massage, leg massage, etc.

Use whirlpool baths, water play, play with mud, clay, sand, etc. Even for older students.

If such routines are ritualized into the day—the quieter ones can be done in the most rigid class setting—they will serve to channelize a great deal of emotion and activity and will cause the remainder of the day to be quieter. If more rambunctious kids are still excited by routines, there is nothing wrong with continuing them for small groups or all, so long as the kids are interested. They will enhance academic skills more reliably than academic drill!

PHYSICAL AND EMOTIONAL DEVELOPMENT: A ROUTINE FOR PHYSICAL DEVELOPMENT

The psychokinetic exercises are best given before breakfast, daily, at least five times a week in the residential setting. They are best done at about 10 A.M. in the day setting, and ad lib in other therapy settings. They can be interchanged with drownproofing, confidence courses, woods and hill runs, caving, climbing, and other vigorous activities—but not with team sports or competitive exercises. They should never be intermingled with military type exercises—which, in any case, should not be given, not even to soldiers.

It is important that the leader of the exercises be as happy, vigorous and joyful as possible without falling into the goody-goody Rover Boys enthusiast model. The routines should be broken up with commands to "Down and Crawl, Bark Like a Dog," "Everybody Crouch and Hop, Cluck Like a Chicken, Crow Like a Rooster," "Quick Find Someone and Hug Em (Boys—Boys, Girls—Girls, or Opposites Only)." The whole procedure should be as lively and as fun as possible.

It is not necessary to use all the routines every day. However, do give the facial exercises, breathing, the puke, and a few each requiring standing, sitting and lying. The order is not critical save that STRETCH AND PUSH should be alternated with SHAKE, HANG LOOSE, AND DROOP.

JUMP-JUMP-BOUNCE-BOUNCE
    hands loosely by side, flopping
    head lolling
    shoulders bouncing

SHOULDERS BACK BOUNCE-BOUNCE
    hands locked behind head
    stretch shoulders back, point elbows back
    bounce back from waist in four rhythm

BEND AT WAIST
(hands remain behind head, elbows back)
rotate elbows, left right left right

BOUNCE BACK
(hands remain behind head)

SWIM
arms extended making swim motions
forwards and backwards

SWIM FLING
as if swimming backwards
fling arms alternatively backwards
fling, fling

WINDMILL
both arms go around at the same time
around around around
reverse

ARMLESS SWIM
hands held loosely up next to breast
shoulders rotated in swim motion

ELBOW TWIST
elbow grasped in opposite hand
twist, pulled over, and bounce with elbow bouncing outside opposite knee
reverse

ELBOW TWIST STRETCH
same as above only pull hard and hold, don't bounce

HORIZONTAL ARM TWIST
arms horizontal, hands flat
bounce full twist left, bounce bounce
bounce, full twist right, bounce bounce
bounce, full twist right, bounce bounce
then do it so your face turns the opposite way

The following photos show several of the facial, breathing, standing, sitting, and lying exercises designed to enhance the physical and emotional development of every child

at Green Valley. The psychokinetic exercises help the child become more aware of his body, relax muscle tension, and relieve inner anxiety.

TOE TOUCH

bouncing down to touch toes, bounce bounce
working to palms flat on ground
spread feet if necessary

TOUCH TOUCH SPREAD

spread feet each few bounces further and further
bounce hands further and further back between legs

STRETCH BOUNCE

fingers laced, hands stretched fully above head, s-t-r-e-t-c-h
fully stretched bounce, bounce
lean back and bounce from waist, s-t-r-e-t-c-h

ROUND THE WORLD

hands still stretched, lean all the way forward
around slowly to the right, back left, forward, several times
reverse—keep stretching

PUSH AWAY THE SUN

push right palm up as hard as possible
push away the sun, push, push, push
left palm
reverse—repeat

CRANE STRETCH

standing, reach back and grasp the right foot in the right hand, lift
  the foot back
lean forward, lift the head back
raise the left hand palm flat up and stretched
stretch and balance
hold and then hop around
reverse and increase the time of holds, then do it with eyes closed

SHAKE SHAKE SHAKE

let everything loose, stand as loosely as possible
flop your hands
flop your arms

SHAKE SHAKE SHAKE (*Continued*)

flop your head
flop your shoulders
flop your middle
flop your right leg
flop your left leg

LUNGE AND LIFT

extend your right hand like a sword fighter
slow motion lunge extending your right foot
go all the way forward on both hands—further
lift your left leg, point the foot
lift up on your fingers, your right foot and lift your head up as high
   as possible
relax, left again
reverse

BRIDGE

both hands and feet extended
drop your pelvis
push head and shoulders up
extend toes so that weight is on top of them
reverse so that pelvis and buttocks are pushed up
arch back upward
reverse, reverse, reverse

SEAL

on your face
extend arms out from body
lift head and torso with arms swinging out tautly
at the same time lift feet and legs leaving body balanced on pelvis
make an explosive 'euh' like a seal as you go up
drop, repeat several times then go up and hold it
repeat

"Increasing the enjoyment of other people is one of the most effective means of recreating socially constructive behavior in troubling youngsters."

"From earliest kindergarten through adult programs we have enjoyed a great deal of success by institutionalizing, ritualizing and programming, increasing physical contact with self and others."

LEG LIFT BACK

    on your face

    place arms along side body palms down

    face turned to side

    lift legs way up

    do it with palms up

LEG LIFT FRONT

    on your back

    hands behind head

    lift feet 3 inches, hold, relax

    hands along side, palms down (then palms up)

    lift 3 inches, hold, relax

    then each way holding for 30-60 seconds

    then each way lifting the legs as high as possible

    roll over backwards

LEG TWIST

    on your back

    lift the left leg high, point the toe

    spread your arms wide and flat

    turn your face to the left

    lay your left leg over the right, pulled up toward your head as far as
       possible as if you were kicking a football

    reverse

    pair off and do this exercise, bending the knee of the leg up and
       having the partner gently push shoulders one way, the knee flat
       across the other leg, reverse and reverse partners

FOOT ROLL

    sit with legs stretched out in front

    roll the feet from heel to toe

    toes out

    toes in

    toes out

    toes in

FOOT POINT/PUSH

sit with legs stretched out in front
point the toes—harder
push the heels—harder
point/push
point/push

PARTNERS SQUEEZE

pair off
sit facing one another
one partner's knees inside the other
outside pushes in
inside pushes out
push push squeeze squeeze
reverse

PARTNERS PULL/PUSH

pair off
sit facing one another
soles of the feet against each other
lock fingers in a hook grasp
pull against the hands
push against the feet
pull/push, keep it up
relax, do it again

PARTNERS SIT UPS

pair off
one partner flat on back
hands locked behind the head
other partner sits on and holds feet down
active partner sits up
twists and touches right elbow to left knee
lies down
sits up, twists and touches left elbow to right knee
repeat twenty times—once or twice half sit, raising 6 inches and
    hold
reverse partners

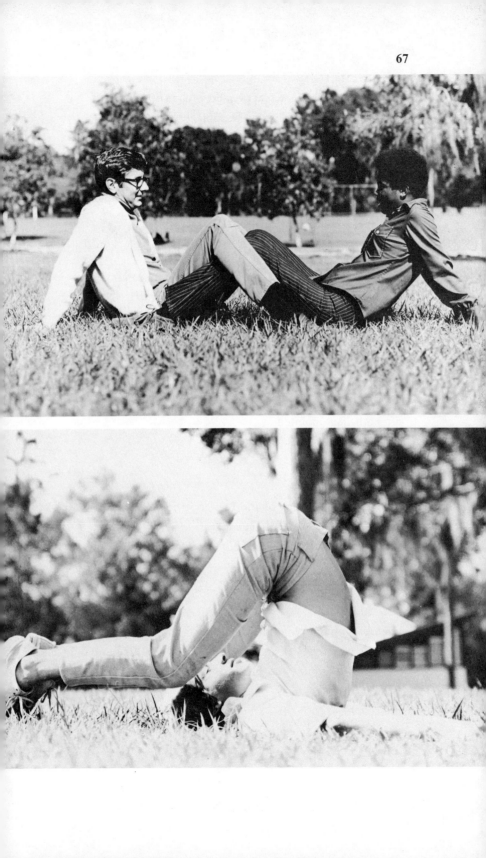

THIGH STRETCH

sit with the soles of the feet pressed to each other

pull the feet in as close as possible

push with hands against the knees

and bounce bounce bounce, the knees down

in the same sitting position raise up so that you are sitting on the
outside edge of your feet, butt clear off the ground (most will
have to cheat with the hands a little) then

bounce bounce bounce

STRETCH AND POINT

seated with the legs stretched out

point the toes

reach down with the hands and grasp the feet in the middle

relax the left leg (still grasping it)

keeping the right leg straight lift it up with the right hand and point
it up

reverse

lift both legs, pointed

roll over backwards

repeat

SEATED TWIST

seated with the soles of the feet together

grasp right elbow in left hand

twist to the left extending the elbow past the knee

stretch

reverse/repeat

BACK BRIDGE

stretched out on your back

work up with the heels until the whole body is lifted and only heels
and head support the body

stretch up

relax

sit up and touch toes

repeat

HULA ROLL

on feet slightly spread
roll the pelvis smoothly
forward, right, back, left, forward, etc.

HULA JERK

on feet slightly spread
push pelvis forward, right, back, left, forward, etc., make motion
   exaggerated/reverse
also right left right left and forward back, etc.

STRETCH BOUNCE

ROUND THE WORLD

SHAKE SHAKE SHAKE

THE PUKE

everything loose
lean way forward
head loose, face loose, mouth loose, tongue loose
shoulders loose, fingers loose, everything loose
now give a big retch
again five or six times, with two or three long holding retches
bounce bounce bounce

ROLL THE NECK

let the neck be loose, flop head forward
roll it to the right, back, left, forward, etc.
reverse
very loose

HEAD PUSH BACK

fingers laced behind head
push back as hard as you can
push push push 10 seconds

ROLL THE NECK

HEAD PUSH FORWARD

fingers laced before forehead
push forward as hard as you can
push push push 10 seconds

ROLL THE NECK

SQUINCH THE FACE

tighten the forehead muscles
eyes, face, squeeze every muscle in your face
tight tight—10 seconds

STRETCH THE FACE

open eyes wide stretch, open mouth
stretch stretch—10 seconds

YAWN

big yawn, bigger, big, big
at least six

DROOP FORWARD

everything loosely forward as in the puke
droop droop (gentle bounce)
droop backwards

TURN ON TO AIR

fingers up as if holding a cigarette
purse the lips
suck in air like smoking very hard and loooooong
fill up, fill up, fill up
let last one be longest you can hold it
AND BLOW IT ALL OUT ALL AT ONCE

DROOP DROOP DROOP

KISS KISS

pooch lips out as far as they will go
push push kiss kiss
relax
now open the mouth as wide as you can—wider—wider
kiss kiss, etc.

NECK/PECTS STRETCH
pull the muscles from the corner of the mouth down through the
  pectorals as tight as possible
stretch, relax, stretch, relax, etc.
bring your hands up about your breasts and feel the stretch
do just the right side
do just the left side
again

EAT THE APPLE
extend a hand as if it held an apple—a big one
bring the hand slowly toward you as you open your mouth for a
  BIG BITE
bite the apple, slow, tautly
again, now do it without the hand as if it were an enemy you were
  biting
big bite, GROWL, SNARL
now clench your fists as you bite
raise them up and sling them down forcefully
AS YOU BITE AND GROWL
bite, growl, and jump like a gorilla all at once
HARDER, ANGRIER

ROLL THE NECK

LOVE THE KNEE
sit and pull up your right knee
hug it as hard as you can
squeeze
reverse
then reverse again and caress your knee
talk to it
tell it you love it
reverse
rub it voluptuously all over

LOVE THE TOE
    take off your shoes
    take your left foot in right hand
    touch the great toe to your nose
    touch the heel to your forehead—see if it will go behind the head
    hold the foot in front of your face and rub the big toe
    caress it, talk to it
    rub it all over
    other foot

LOVE THE SELF
    still seated start vigorously scratching your head
    keep going, rub your face
    then go all over your body vigorously rubbing
    tell yourself how nice each part is, love yourself
    right down to the toes
    start again at the head rubbing with open palms gently, slowly,
        roundly and voluptuously, all over
    then massage each arm and shoulder, pectorals and breasts
    side and back
    thighs, calves and feet
    then gently slap up and down your thighs, inside and out
    harder
    then gently slap face and back of neck
    harder
    while seated, lace fingers and stretch above your head

PARTNERS MASSAGE
    have each partner massage the other
    backs, legs, arms, all the great muscles
    gentle back slap
    if you have balance bars or are indoors with walls have the partner
        gently walk up the legs and back of the other, heels opposite on
        each side of the spine, toes out and up, slowly shuffling
    have stronger boys (some girls) stand on each others' stomachs

gently push with feet at shoulder muscles
thigh muscles

PARTNERS LIFT
    have one partner stand at the feet of the other
    lean over and grasp hands pulling up prone partner who remains as
        stiff and straight as possible
    up and down
    reverse
    have three individuals of two partners lift the fourth and carry
        about
    exchange until all are lifted
    have five individuals of a group of three partners lift the sixth as
        high as possible and carry about, exchange until all are lifted

SCRAMBLE
    as fast as possible following the command of the leader
    ON YOUR FACE
    ON YOUR BACK
    ON YOUR FACE
    SIT
    RUN RUN RUN (IN PLACE)
    ON YOUR FACE
    BOUNCE BOUNCE BOUNCE
    RIGHT SIDE
    SQUAT
    ON YOUR BACK
    LEFT SIDE
    SIT
    ETC.

the routine would always be ended with

BITE, JUMP, GROWL,
SCRAMBLE
BOUNCE, BOUNCE, BOUNCE

or some other vigorous and happy activity

A ROUTINE FOR RELAXATION AND AWARENESS

In general we find the usual relaxation routine to be useless with adolescents. The suggestion "relax" seems to operate with Tom Sawyer effect, and merely focuses attention on the anxiety the child has about his body. We have found that a routine that compels attention, without suggestion or command for relaxation, is more widely applicable. We have also used this routine for "training" expectant mothers for childbirth without anesthesia or pain (with slightly different wording at the end of the routine).

This routine can be given after a session of the psychokinetic exercises. In this case the exercises will probably (but not necessarily) be given indoors, and might simply include the seated and lying exercises, without the vigorous and enthusiastic exercises otherwise used toward the end of the session in which the children are instructed to follow the leader without verbal commands. Other routines can be added as suggested by the basic routine.

Thirty minutes seems sufficient for the routine and should be followed by ten minutes or so of rest or ad lib behavior so long as it is quiet. It is vastly preferable that the teacher not read the routine. The order of presentation is not important so long as the leader does not go over the body from head to toe, vice versa, or in any readily discernable pattern. The presentation should be random. The directions should be given as fluently and naturally as possible and can be tape recorded.*

The students should be as comfortable as possible, ideally in reclining chairs with head and knees supported. If they are lying, flat, pillows should preferably support the head and knees. If the group is too large or facilities are not available simply instruct the group to lie about as they wish in as comfortable a position as they can find.

"I want you to close your eyes and rest as comfortably as you can.

"As you listen to me I want you to think about your big toe. Just think about it and feel it as you lie there. If you can't feel it from inside just lying there, reach down and rub it.

*Tape sold by *Humanitas*

"Now think about the very top of your head. As you lie there feel the top of your head, think yourself right up into your scalp, BE the top of your head. If you can't feel it from inside, reach up and scratch it good.

"Think about your chin, the very tip of your chin. As you lie there feel the tip of your chin, think yourself right into the tip of your chin, INHABIT the tip of your chin. If you can't feel it from inside, reach up and rub it hard.

"Feel your right knee cap, feel the top of it, and the edges and the way it connects to your leg. Squeeze yourself all down into that right knee cap, BE your right knee cap. If you can't feel it from inside, reach down and rub it hard.

"Notice your left ear. Can you feel the inside of it? Reach up and rub it if you can't feel all of it.

"Think about the outside corner of your left eye, feel the way it pulls into your temple. Feel the flesh at the top of your eye. Around your left eye. The eye lid. Under the eye. Feel the way it comes up to the bridge of your nose. If you can't feel it reach up and rub it good.

"Think about the sole of your right foot, feel the way it curves into the ball of your right foot, feel how the ball separates into the toes. Think into your little toe. The second toe. Can you feel it? If you can't reach down and wiggle it good. The middle toe. Wiggle it. The fourth toe. Feel your great toe. Wiggle it. Tense it. Tense your whole right foot. Let go. Inhabit that foot. Feel it feel the way it goes up into your ankle. The tendon at the back. The cord that pulls. Point your toes. Now feel that cord at the back. Push your heel. Now let go. Feel your right foot.

"Is your left shoulder there? Feel it. Move it. Feel in your left arm pit. Can you feel the way the shoulder slants up to the neck? Can you feel your left ear? Is your left eye still there? Move your left shoulder around. Feel the shoulder blade. Notice how the shoulder fits on your back. Feel the way your arm comes down from it. Stretch the arm out. Let it down. Feel your upper left arm. INHABIT the upper arm. Slide down into the left elbow. Feel the under arm. Feel the forearm. Feel the front and the muscle. Think about the back and the long bone. Feel where it joins the thumb. Can you feel your left thumb? The ball of the thumb. The joints. The pointed end. The nail. Stretch your left fingers. Let loose. Feel the index finger. Feel the space between it and the next. Feel all the spaces between your left fingers. Feel your index finger. Really feel it. Get inside it. Be that index finger. Feel the middle finger. The ring finger. The little finger. Think about the cutting edge of the hand down from the little finger. Feel your wrist. Move it around. Tense all the muscles of your left hand and arm. Now the shoulder. Let go.

"Is your stomach there? Feel your stomach. Feel right where it starts under your ribs. Feel the bottom ribs, then feel the start of your stomach. Feel how it lies all around in the cavity of your body. Feel how it settles at the base against your pelvis. Feel the skin on the outside. Feel your belly button. Is it there? Rub it once if you can't feel it. Stick a finger in it and rub around. Can you feel how your stomach vees down between your legs into your genitals? Feel the top of your stomach. The middle. The bottom. Now the right side. Feel the way it slopes to the right under the ribs. Are you breathing? Can you feel your breath move your ribs and push your stomach? Feel how your side goes down into your back.

"Purse your lips. Pooch them out like a funny kiss. Now just feel them. Feel the upper lip. Feel the edges, how it comes inside your mouth. Feel inside your upper lip in front of the teeth. Feel the corners of your mouth. The left. The right. Feel inside your lower lip. Feel the way your teeth push against your lip. Is your tongue there? Can you feel it? Move it around. Touch your teeth with it. Feel the last tooth way back on the bottom on the left side. Now follow the teeth around to the front slowly around to the right and all the way back. Now up to the teeth all the way on the right. Slowly around to the front, and back to the left all the way to the back. Can you feel the whole inside of your mouth? Your throat? The top of your mouth. Down your neck inside. The front of your neck. If you can't feel it from inside reach up and rub it. Feel the way it moves down into your spine, the long slope of your back bone?

"Make a fist with your right hand. Squeeze it tight. Squeeze your right arm too. All of it. The shoulder. Squeeze, and squinch up the right side of your face. Squeeze your right side too. Squeeze squeeze. Add your right leg. Squeeze everything on your right side. And let go.

"Are you breathing? Just lie there and hear and feel yourself breathe. Are you? Do you feel your ribs? Your stomach? Your right foot?

"Feel your right eye. Squeeze it shut hard. Harder. Relax. Can you feel the inside corner? Follow it under, the outside corner, up, and back along your eyebrow. Can you feel your eyebrow? Reach up and scratch it. Squeeze up your forehead. Feel your forehead and let it relax. Just feel all your forehead. The top of your head from front to back. The back of your head. The back of your neck. All the way down your backbone between your shoulder blades. The small of your back. Your left side. The soft part of your left side between your ribs and your hip. Your right hip. Your left hip. Feel the way your left hip moves into your pelvis. Feel your whole pelvis. Sense the way your body sits in it.

"Feel the way your right leg fits into your body. Feel the butt underneath. The joint above. The side of your hip and thigh. The inside of your thigh, where it joins the body, down to your knee. Your right knee. Feel the joint. Feel the right knee cap. Feel its edges, it joins to the leg. Think down your shin. The outside of the right leg. Your right calf. The ankle joint. Push out your right heel. Relax. Feel the sole of your right foot.

"Feel your backbone between the shoulder blades. Feel the way your ribs come into it. Feel out from your backbone on both sides and feel the swell of your ribs, out to your rib sides, over, to the front, feel your whole chest, and feel yourself breathe. Feel the breath push against your stomach. And feel the whole front of your chest. Feel the meat along the side of your chest. Your muscles coming down from your shoulders. Feel the skin over your chest. Your breasts. The lift of ribs at the bottom of your chest. The skin pulling up from the bottom of your chest. The curve at the bottom of your breasts. The lift of flesh. Your right nipple. Feel the way the cloth rubs against the nipple. Your left nipple. Feel the way your skin and flesh falls away from the nipple. Feel your chest coming up to your collarbone. Feel your right collarbone. Your left collarbone. Feel the way the soft hollow comes just above it. Feel your throat. Swallow. Are you breathing?

"Feel your left butt. Feel the way it rounds into the separation of yourself. Feel how the separation comes up to the bone below the small of your back. Feel the side of your right butt along the separation. Think along the separation, deep inside, from the small of your back, along past your rectum, forward to your genitals. Feel the way your genitals grow into your body. Sense the covering, sense the inside.

"Are you breathing? Feel your ribs move, the pressure against your stomach. Feel your throat. Feel your mouth. Your jaw. The muscles in your right jaw, your left. Your teeth. The inside of your mouth. The very tip of your nose. Back along the bridge of your nose. Your right nostril. Your left. The sides of your nose. The way it joins your right cheek, your right cheek all along the bottom of your eye, the middle of your cheek. Pooch it out with air. Feel the back of your jaw as it hinges to your head. Feel your left cheek. All around. Pooch it out. Feel your mouth blow out the air. Wiggle your jaw.

"Tense up your left leg. All of it. Foot. Toes. Butt. Thigh. Side muscles. Back muscles on the left. Left shoulder. Left arm and hand. Left side of neck. Face. Squeeze. Relax.

"Now feel yourself breathe. Feel the air coming in your nose, let some in your mouth. Feel it go down your throat. Feel it into your lungs. Feel your ribs. Chest. Stomach. Feel all your stomach. Feel it inside.

"Now tense yourself all over. Head. Neck. Face. Shoulders. Arms and hands. Side. Stomach. Thighs. Back. Calves. Feet and toes.

Tense everything tighter and tighter. Squeeze. Squeeze. Relax. Let everything all loose.

"Now feel the top of your head. Inhabit the top of your head. Let yourself just BE inside the top of your head. Now slide slowly down your forehead. Your eyes. Cheeks. Nose. Mouth. Chin. Under your chin. Neck. Chest. Ribs. Breasts. Stomach. Pubic Bone. Genitals. Thighs. Knees, Shins. Ankle. Top of feet. Toes. Let yourself seem to flow out of your toes and let the feeling and awareness stream from the top of your head to the end of your toes all the way down yourself from head to toes.

"Feel into your big toes. Focus on those big toes. Concentrate on the big toes. Inhabit your big toes. BE nothing but your big toes. Now notice the other toes. Flow back to the balls of your feet. The arches and soles. The heels. The cord. Back up your calves. The inside of your knees. The back of your thighs. Your butts. The separation between them. The small of your back. The meat along your backbone. All up your backbone, the back of your shoulders. The back of your neck. The back of your head, the very top of your head. Let the feeling seem to flow from your toes all the way up through everything to the top of your head. Feel all of yourself from the tip of your big toes back through yourself to the top of your head."

(At this point the whole routine can be repeated, or a portion of it, or just the last serial inventory, depending on the teacher's sense of the relaxation and participation of the children.)

"Now as you lie there I want you to imagine that you are lying on the grass in a warm, sunlit garden, all green, all golden, all warm from the light of the sun. The garden has a nice stone wall around it and no one can see in and you are all warm and alive and relaxed and safe lying on the grass in the golden, green, warm sunlit garden. And you see yourself walking around in the garden all tall and alive, and warm and safe and at ease in the warm sunlit garden and you feel the sun all over you in the garden. You walk all around in the warm sunlit garden, alive, golden, warm, round, relaxed, safe, protected, all alone in the nice sunlit gentle warm, kind green garden under the golden light of the sun. And you fall softly and safely and gently to sleep in the golden green garden under the golden light of the sun. And you fall softly and safely and gently to sleep in the golden green warm garden. And you are all soft and safely asleep in the garden with the warm wall and the safe sun shining on you in the green warm golden garden."

(The routine can be stopped at this point. The children should have been told before that when the voice stops they may rest or may quietly go about. When activity resumes it should, of course, initially be very quiet, safe and fragile.)

(The routine can be extended, either on the first session or by steps in each subsequent session. Extension may be merely amplifying the last garden sketch, or by adding the sketches below and any others. The routine may also be used for staging a different kind of outcome by the projective routines below, or by the routines for expectant mothers below.)

"And when you've slept in the nice, warm, safe, round, golden garden with the sun shining all over you safely stretched on the soft grass in the safe walled garden you wake and you walk around all alive, and warm, all alive and safe, all alive and at home in the warmth and safety of the garden and you walk from the garden into the house and sit in front of a big big window in a big comfortable chair and you rest in the chair all comfortable and at ease and warm and relaxed and happy and safe in the cozy warm house looking out at the blue sky all lighted and warm by the sun with the tall white round warm clouds floating gently in the sky and the breeze softly blowing as you sit looking in the warm, comfortable chair in the cozy warm house in the dark of the warm soft safe room sitting all relaxed and drowsy in the soft comfortable chair and as you watch the tall white round warm clouds you sit in the warm soft comfortable chair and you fall gently and softly and warmly and safely asleep and you sleep in the chair."

(The routine can be ended here, or the two sketches can be repeated, or the last, or other sketches can be added, either for attention/relaxation, projection of ideas and feelings, or the special routines for pregnancy.)

"And as you sleep in the soft warm comfortable chair all warm and safe and relaxed and drowsy safely sleeping in the comfortable chair you slowly and easily and gently wake up and stretch all over feeling yourself stretch all alive and awake all over and you stand out of the chair and you walk out of the house down a nice wooded hill with the breezes all gently blowing warmly by you and the sun warming the green trees and the blue sky rounds above you with the white warm round clouds softly floating and you walk to a blue blue beach all curved into the distance all curved and round and the soft wind blowing gently round and round and waves gently rushing up to the soft sand that you feel under your feet as the golden sun warmly shines all over your body and you stretch and feel the wind against your skin as it is warmed all over by the bright of the golden sun and the waves rush gently in and the beach curves in the distance and closes you in with the water and the clouds and the golden sun warming in the blue sky with the soft beach against your feet and you stretch and run in the bright of the sun warming your skin and the warm wind blows all over you as the waves rush gently in against the beach and the waves and the wind and the beach close round you all safe and warm and alive and tingling and relaxed and loose and waves blowing the wind gently as the sun brightly warms your body as you stretch all tingly all alive all warm all safe all round all close and gentled and safe and relaxed and easy and the waves roll in softly, warmly, roundly, rushingly, easily, safely, rushing, across the water, as the sun, brightly, warmingly, safely, gentles, the air, the water, the waves, the wind, the clouds, as you all alive, all relaxed, all tingly, all refreshed, all extended to the sun, to the waves, to the wind, to the beach, to the safety of the world, alive, alive, rush and leap and play and enjoy all alive on the beach as the waves rush in through the golden light of the sun on the warm sand of the beach as it closes gently and safely around you and you live in the sun."

(The routine can be ended here, repeated, all three repeated, or any variation. The routine can be extended by the projective routines or the pregnancy routines.)

"And you see yourself all asleep in your bed. Softly and warmly and gently and roundly asleep in your bed. And you imagine that you come out of yourself, all feeling yourself as you come out of yourself from toes up out of the top of your head. And you feel yourself lift up out of yourself and stream and fly and lift and stream and fly up out of your window all extended and tingly and alive and glorious and you fly way up into the sky all warm and safe and alive and you can see all around and see and see and you fly and you fly and you fly. And you can feel yourself extend all the way back to yourself in your bed all safe and warm and round and comfy in your bed all snuggled and warm and covered and easy in your bed as you gloriously fly into the sky all electric and extended and alive and all safe and contained and you can see all around and you see and you see and you see. And you feel yourself coming back feeling into yourself all streaming back into the top of your head and you are all safe and warm and comfy and round and warm and asleep in your bed. And you are all round and safe and warm and comfy and covered snuggly all safe and warm in your bed and sleep all warm in your bed. And you sleep all safe in your bed. And you sleep all loose in your bed. And you sleep in your bed."

Projective routines merely add to the sketches above, situations into which the pupil can project his own imagining without the detail being given by the teacher. To some extent the sketches are already built in a fashion. In the garden for instance, "And as you walk in the garden you hear the gate open and your very best friend comes in and you play and play." *Or,* "As you sleep in the garden a nice grown-up comes in and gently and softly wakes you up." "As you play in the garden you see a *Life* magazine lying on the grass and you see someone you know on the cover." *It is not useful for the teacher to try to determine who or what the child sees in these situations. It is enough that the child gets a framework from the teacher in which to*

*fantasize, that the framework is given in the approved social setting
of the classroom and established by a respected authority. It is also
useful that the fantasy is set in safety after a great deal of work to
create relaxation and comfort. As the child moves along with the
routines very mildly stressful situations can be introduced.* "Someone
you don't like, but it is all right because it is your magic garden where
you are warm and safe and golden in the bright light of the sun all safe
and round and tingly and stretched up to the warmth of the sun all
over you." "And you hear the school bell ringing but it is. . . ." "And
you hear a car's brake suddenly squeal over the wall, but it is .

All of these routines are of course equally useful with adults.

Questions will be raised by many teachers whose own sensi-
bilities are offended by the frank enjoyment of the body subsumed by
these routines. Other teachers will believe the routines are acceptable to themselves but could not be used in their own settings. All
that we can say to these questions is the maximization of human
beings depends on all of their sensations and perceptions being
available freely to them. If they are to enjoy full control and direction
of themselves they must be able to perform with all the data. If
anyone thinks that chastity is going to be built effectively on denial of
the flesh, which in our religious view is the Temple of God, then that
person ought to reflect on the fact that prostitution, homosexuality,
sexual assault, perversions and rape flourish in the so-called Christian
civilizations while among "savages" like the Trobriand Islanders, who
relaxedly enjoy their God-given flesh in the joys of the sun, homosexuality is unknown, strictly practiced monogamy is the rule, and
the idea of prostitution is a kind of incomprehensible joke.

When these routines are used with expectant mothers the internal feelings around the abdomen, lower back and genitals must be
emphasized. The teacher can simply record descriptions and present
them without any preliminary discussion of the issue. Most girls and
women accept the authority of the teaching and clinical situation and
accept the directions in a quite matter of fact way. The usefulness of
the routines will be enhanced if a more organic and direct language is

used. Words like vagina, labia, genitals, pubic mound, etc., can usefully be used with upper middle class women, or women with college training. But these terms do not enjoy a very great currency among other classes, and certainly not among the kind of child who generally is sent for residential service as an unwed mother.

If the teacher has problems with this area it may be better to have a brief discussion with the girls giving them the appropriate terminology in the context of a sexual hygiene class. Otherwise a simple straightforward use of the more gentle of the common or vulgar terminology will be the only responsible thing to do.

CHILDBIRTH ROUTINE

"As you feel yourself breathing you feel the push of your belly against your ribs and you feel the round of your stomach all firm and round and solid in you. You feel the push of your belly against your ribs and you feel it all round and heavy in yourself.

"You feel the weight of your belly against your back, and settling into pelvis and hips and you feel the round of you. You feel the pull of your skin across your stomach, you feel it tightening as you breathe and you feel your breath as it pushes against you.

"As you feel yourself breathing you feel inside of yourself all warm and liquid, all solid and heavy, all round and warm in you. You feel how right and how solid your tummy fits in you. Feel the weight of it against your back and feel how it settles against your pelvis and hip.

"As you feel the roundness of yourself inside yourself you can feel how you fit down into yourself, how you fit into your pelvis and how the baby inside you fits down into you and into the seat of yourself as it weighs itself into your pelvis.

"Feel the inside of your thighs, feel how they spread from the separation of you, you can feel how they stretch from the middle of you, how they open and spread from you. Feel how they come together at the join of you and how the weight of the child in you gently weighs against the cradle of your pelvis and how easily and readily the opening of you waits for the child. You can feel how the heaviness of your belly leads down into the opening of you.

"Feel the separation of you. Feel from the weight of you on your butts deep into the separation of you. Sense the rectum in the middle of you and how you flow up into the separation of you into the lips of your vagina, and the surface and skin and covering of your pubis. Sense yourself in your pubis, in the separation of yourself, in the opening and lips of your vagina, into the opening and passage of your sex. Feel the rightness of you as the weight of your belly above pushes against you and you sense the flow of you down into your genitals and the opening of you out through the passage and the lips of your sex and the spread and the weight of your thighs.

"As you feel yourself breathing you feel the push of your stomach against your ribs, you feel the roundness of your belly inside yourself, you sense the presence and the rightness of the child in you, you feel the weight and the promise of the life in you. Feel the weight of yourself against your back. Feel the weight of yourself against yourself inside against your backbone. Feel the heaviness of yourself and the rightness of yourself fit firmly and roundly into the seat of yourself into your pelvis. Feel how the weight and feeling of yourself flows down in your belly, in your pelvis, in the middle and center of you, into the spreading of you, into the passage of your sex, the flow of you through the lips of your vagina, the separation of you, the spread and weight of your thighs. Feel the rightness of you, the ripeness, the fertility and promise of you, feel the sense of you in your sex, the sense of you in your belly, feel the being of you in your thighs, feel the strength of you in the small of your back.

"Feel the weight of you against your butts. Feel the small of your back. Inhabit the small of your back. Feel the bone below. The spread of the butts. The crevice that separates you. Sense the depths of you, the rectum deep in the crevice of you, the spread of you up to your sex, the depths of the passage of you, the opening into yourself inside your pelvis the weight and roundness of yourself upholding the roundness and weight of yourself as the weight and solidity and ripeness of your child fills you."

This sketch should come in a sequence in which the garden sketch follows the first inventories, then this sketch is followed by the beach sketch, this sketch is repeated and the beach sketch follows again with great care given to producing a soft, rhythmical and gentle presentation.

EXERCISES FOR ENHANCING CONTACT AND AWARENESS

A number of the techniques discussed in this handbook will build perception of self contact with the external world, and more vivid awareness. This is particularly true of the techniques discussed in Chapter Two.

The particular techniques discussed here are best used with more intelligent and cooperative pupils as assignments. That is, the children are given a card on which the exercise is described as well as by participating with the class in a tape recorded or teacher directed session.

The exercises that follow ought to be labeled for the class with some easily recognized term. They should be ritualized into the day in the rhythm of quiet and inwardness so that the children move easily and naturally into them.

LOOK AND LOOK

GENERAL DIRECTIONS: for five minutes or so focus your attention first on something near you, look at it thoroughly, see how it fits against its background, look at all the parts of it, think about it as it might be upside down or some other way. Then quickly shift to something far away and do the same thing. Then close. Then far away. Then in the middle distance. Remark on whether you persist or start to day-dream or forget the procedure. Do you stop on one object? How do you feel?

DESCRIPTIVE DIRECTIONS: "I want you to play LOOK AND LOOK with me. I want you to hold quite still and quiet for a little time and without moving your heads very much at all look at the thing I say. Look as hard as you can and see everything about it that you can.

"Look at something on your desk (or on your lap), look at it closely. See how it is put together, notice how it looks against the things in back of it. Focus right on it and see how the things around and behind it sort of disappear.

"Now look at the picture on the far wall. Look at it closely. See all the parts of it. Notice how the things in between it and you sort of disappear as you focus on the picture. Look at how it lies against the wall.

"Now look at your right little finger. See how it joins your hand. See where it lies against the next finger. Look at all the details of it. Look closer. See the little pores in your skin. Look at your finger holding it up against the back wall. Now look at the picture again. Look at the finger. Look at the wall around the picture.

"Now look at the desk. Pick out the vase on the desk. Look at the flower in the vase. See the way the stem comes into the vase from the flower. Glance at all the other things on the desk. Now go back to the flower. See if you can see all the petals. Now look back at your little finger. The picture on the wall. Your finger. The flower. The desk. The front of your dress or shirt. The wall."

The teacher can continue this kind of routine for about five minutes. The point is to encourage awareness of the different structures in the way we organize our looking. Children with glasses should be encouraged to take them off unless their vision is too poor even to see the picture framed on the wall. The teacher may expect some emotional expression as the simple exercise goes on and should support it as long as it remains personal.

LISTEN, LISTEN!

GENERAL DIRECTIONS: for five minutes or so focus your attention on a sound, try to tell where it is coming from, how it is made, listen to all the parts of it, find out if it is made of more than one simple sound. Then shift to another sound. Try to be aware of the first sound and any others while you focus on the second sound. Try to tell where it is coming from, how it is made. Listen to all the parts of it. Then shift to another sound. Be aware of all the relations of all the sounds around you but focus on one sound at a time.

DESCRIPTIVE DIRECTIONS: "I want you to play LISTEN, LISTEN! with me. While we are quite still and quiet I want you to listen to the thing I say. Listen as hard as you can and hear everything about the sound there is to hear.

"Listen to the cricket out the window. Listen to how his sound changes. . . .

"Now listen to the far away truck. Do you still hear the cricket? But focus on the truck. Can you hear how it changes? . . .

"Hear the clock ticking. Listen to the ticking of the clock. Can you hear all of the clock's sound? What happened to the cricket and the truck. Can you hear all three?

"Listen to the tree rustling in the wind."

The teacher can continue these descriptions, focusing on new sounds, returning to the old and drawing attention to the changes in relationships and structures, without calling them by any abstract name. The teacher must only suggest the direction of awareness and organization, point; never build a verbal wall around sensation.

FEELY, FEELY

GENERAL DIRECTIONS: for five minutes or so focus your attention on the way things feel on your skin. The way you feel as your weight presses on the chair. The feel of feet in shoes and against the floor. The places where clothing is tight—waist, crotch, under arms, elbows, knees. Can you feel any draft? Are some places warmer or colder than others? Do you itch or twinge anywhere? Now reach out and touch different things. Touch them not only with your hands, but with the softer skin near your elbow, with your face and forehead, taste some things.

In giving descriptive directions to a class try to have available a richer than usual array of artifacts and textured surfaces. Try to suggest awareness of the original set of feelings as they try the new sensations, reaching out. That is, you are still sitting in the chair and touching the floor, your clothes still touch you, the breeze still blows all the while you focus on other feelings. Suggest attention to them while more strongly directing focus on one feeling so that the pupils can construct the relationships for themselves.

TASTE TIME

GENERAL DIRECTIONS: for five minutes or so focus your attention on the way several mouthsful of food feel, change and taste. Try not to talk to yourself as you do this. Feel the texture of the food with tongue, lips, teeth and mouth. Try the difference between bland and soft foods and crisp and tasty foods. Toward the end of the exercise take one bite of a solid food and chew it, focusing your awareness on it all the time until it is liquified. Don't swallow it until it is absolutely liquified. Focus your attention on the whole process all the while.

The teacher should see that several bite sized bits of food are available, or a carrot, an apple, a raw turnip or other food with substance. The liquification is usefully done with a piece of solid meat. The teacher should be very gentle and quiet in giving these directions.

SOUND MIRROR

Take about five inches of tape from your recorder and splice it so it is a complete loop (a little experiment will show you the ideal size loop for your recorder). This loop will drive through the recording and playback heads without being on the spools. Have the pupils individually make a statement, or sounds (progressively encourage them to make sounds, particularly emotional sounds; retching is very powerful and they enjoy the whole procedure very much), and let them play over and over again about ten times for each. Then instruct the pupils to sit quietly and see if they can remember sounds without the tape recorder. Remind them that their heads are really good recorders and tell them to sit quietly and try to think and remember sounds as closely as possible. See if they are hi-fi.

MIRROR MIRROR

Bring a good sized mirror (12" x 12") to class and make each student look into it. Have them look without any comment at all for 30 seconds or so. Then ask them to tell you what they see. Force more and more description out of them in a gentle but insistent way. When it gets very difficult shift to another. Keep the pace fast.

If you have a closed circuit TV recorder system, record the child doing a very simple thing: sitting in a chair, turning around, squatting to the floor, making faces, stretching or just standing, for about 30 seconds. Immediately play it back. Have the child describe in great detail everything he sees. If your equipment will hold a frame, stop the picture and have him thoroughly discuss what he sees. Or take a Polaroid picture during the action. If you don't have a TV system use a Polaroid.

MEMORY TIME

When the pupils are quieted, either after an awareness/relaxation tape or otherwise, play Memory. "I want you to sit quietly, close your eyes if you like, and remember something very very nice that happened to you. Remember everything about it. How did it look, who was there, what were they wearing, what did it smell like, was it cold or hot, what did you have on, who was nearest you. . . ."

As your relationship with the pupils goes on and their quiet periods are more reliably relaxed, slowly introduce other themes. Ask them: "Remember a time when you were angry," "when you were excited," "when you were sad," or "when you were frightened."

After they have gotten quite fluent at remembering in these three or four minute exercises suggest that they change the memory: "Remember but then change the memory. Remember it as it wasn't. Remember someone there who wasn't. Pretend you did something different. Remember it as completely different as if everything were opposite. Remember it as if it were a movie running backwards."

After they are quite happy with this kind of remembering, and you have made sure that your daily sessions interchange straight remembering with make-believe changing memories, have them "remember" things that never happened at all. "Make believe you are remembering something that never happened at all. Remember something that didn't happen to you at all."

NOW

GENERAL DIRECTIONS: As you sit quietly make statements to yourself about exactly what you are aware of at this very moment. Make every statement begin with "Now I" or "At this moment I" or "Here and now I." Be aware of as many things as you can. Is your heart beating? Are you breathing? Try doing it with a tape recorder. Try writing down things. Then just talk to yourself. Then try to be aware without talking to yourself. Can you be absolutely silent inside yourself?

In a class this exercise can follow the longer drills or not. The children can be told to write or not if they please. Excellent small tape recorders are readily available. If the pupils do tape or write they should be asked to spend some time just talking to themselves. A later part of the exercise should be for everyone just to sit or lie quietly and see if they can stop talking to themselves at all.

LEFT RIGHT

GENERAL DIRECTIONS: As you sit quietly or lie down sense your body. Make a random inventory. Then begin to compare left against right. Compare the way your right arm settles to the left. The whole side against side. Then try front and back. Inventory each portion. But don't do it in a systematic way. Bounce from point to point. See how each section of your body hangs together and compare it to the other side—left/right, front/back.

TOUCH, TOUCH

GENERAL DIRECTIONS: Move quietly about the room and touch things. Touch at least 20 different things. With the tip of your finger, hand, back of hand, arm, face, forehead, lean up against things. Describe to yourself everything about the thing you are touching and things around it. Note all that you are aware of as you move about. Sit down and touch things. Lie down and touch. Touch other people.

FACES

GENERAL DIRECTIONS: For about five minutes make all the different faces you can. Calm faces. Extreme faces. Feel everything you can about yourself as you make the faces. Then make them into a mirror. Join with a partner and make faces at each other. Carefully look at everything your partner does. How do you think he feels? Think about him feeling as you feel. Think about feeling as he feels. Gather together a small group, not more than 6, and make faces at each other. Make all the same together, then different. Turn your backs to each other in a circle and make faces outward.

BODIES

GENERAL DIRECTIONS: For about five minutes express emotions and actions in as many ways as you can with your body.

Keep checking all your sensations and awareness. Don't forget to communicate to yourself by tensing up everywhere appropriate to what you are expressing. Face a partner and express actions and emotions to him all without talking. Join a small group and express to each other. With a minimum of talking do the same thing, then all different. Turn your backs to each other in a circle and express outward. Sit down and do it. Lie down and do it. Lie down and relax and then express the first emotion that comes to mind.

Any of these drills can be used in association with others or as breaks throughout the day. After the third or fourth time the pupils will learn the name of the routine and quickly join in.

MOVE

GENERAL DIRECTIONS: Sit quietly and then do a simple action focusing on everything that is happening. Get up and walk across the room, return and sit. Get up and lie flat on the floor. Get up and have a glass of water. Get up and open a window and return. Sense all the motions and adjustments. Feel all the various parts of your body as you move.

In a class have each separately do some very simple movement. Then all together. Keep the tone of the room very gentle and very quiet. Suggest awarenesses, but not too many. Allow long pauses.

BLIND

Try to operate for 15 minutes, then 30, then an hour and more while blindfolded. How do you feel? Sit down immediately after and tape or write everything you can remember about it. Next day or several hours later sit quietly and remember as much as possible about the whole experience.

DEAF

Try to operate for 15 minutes and progressively more while your ears are stopped and bound with muffs. Inventory your feelings and awareness. Sit down and write or tape everything you can remember about it. Sit quietly hours or days after and remember each part of the experience in as much detail as possible.

MUTE

How long can you go without saying anything at all? What happens? Can you stop talking inside to yourself? Break the class into groups and say "I want you just to sit and not say anything at all for as long a part of an hour as you possibly can. If you do have to talk then talk about why you have to talk. When the hour is over we'll talk." Then talk about it.

See if the class can go a whole morning or afternoon, or a whole day without any talk at all. Is it easier if they can make grunts and other noises? How do they feel?

HOLDING AND FREEDOM ROOMS

In general we believe that the need for emotional "ventilation" is enormously overemphasized by the psychotherapeutic approach. We have noted that even quite disturbed schizophrenics will respond to abrupt and forceful commands for control. There is no evidence that forcing control is harmful. Still, we see little need for the incredibly complex controls that are exacted from kids. Surely children have better uses for their energies than keeping tight control over noise all day long, sitting decorously, or all the other biologically nonsensical instructions that are the chief effort of ordinary school programs. A teacher who is going about her job of instructing in fundamental intellectual skills like reading, writing and arithmetic ought not be expected to be either a psychotherapist stickily dealing with the whole range of possible emotion, or a drill sergeant teaching foolish and educationally irrelevant skills of robot-like control. Such wasted energies could more properly be applied to reading or playing.

Children sent to us with a "rage" history almost never display it. If they do they are bluntly and firmly stopped. If necessary, a child is firmly, calmly and quietly held in a lap, or however needed, by one or six of the staff if needed. No attempt is made to talk to the child in such a situation, except that younger kids are given soft comforting mama noises. As the adolescent moves from vicious verbal vituperation to sobbing, the same kind of semi-articulate nonrational sounds and statements are made with comforting touches, caresses and holding. Some small children have to be held nightly, usually at, or just after bedtime, for weeks. An older child usually will require a longer single session, but fewer repetitions.

In general, simply holding the child during any extreme emotion will tend to give him overall control rather quickly. While it seems better that the holding be done as gently and in as kindly a way as possible, it is quite often not possible with a strong adolescent. We encourage staff to be as emotionally honest as they can in such a situation, not to attempt to control their verbal responses at all, but to maintain good firm physical control. With such a child, of course, adequate staff is needed. Sometimes a motherly and competent woman teacher, or a gently strong man can achieve the same effect by an almost symbolic holding just grasping a hand or arm. Analytical talk, or focusing talk or judgment talk must be avoided at these times.

In some centers—the Brown Camps most notably—these scenes are precipitated. That is, the children have formal "holding" sessions when they are told they are absolutely safe and they can let go. A mild scene can be accelerated by the intensity of the holding, by rubbing the back and gently pushing at sore spots, by verbal pushing, or by setting a boundary a bit more firmly than absolutely necessary. These processes seem to give the child a larger sense of safety and, in any case, their self-control and freedom from raging quickly occurs. Their general emotional expressiveness increases.

Freedom rooms are based on a similar principle. A room is prepared, either with no windows or reinforced windows and with protected lighting. Preferably the room is padded or walled with wood paneling that has some give. Ideally, small durable upholstered tubes and pillows are available to beat with, bite, throw or any such action. The child is told that he can do anything he wants while he is in the room and some sort of signal is devised to warn him when the adult is entering. The signal is always followed by a pause before the adult enters.

A freedom room seems useful both as an alternative to the required classroom, and in and of itself. Ideally the child should have several free areas to go to if his classroom behavior is difficult, or simply if he wishes to retreat from the classroom. Such environments should never be invested with a sense of punishment. However, the teacher ideally should always be free to say, "Look, Buster, the rest of us want to work, and want to have quiet to do it in. Either shape up or bop on off to the play room (freedom room, playing field, or whatever)." In my experience even very trying children given that kind of blunt alternative settle down and begin to participate. A group may go off for a whole day or more. There is no loss for them since their attention is lost in the classroom anyway and they harm others' learning ability. The gain is in a new moral relationship with the teacher, an opportunity to work off the tension, tautness and arousal that prevents good attention, and a new kind of useful authority in the classroom.

PHYSICAL MANIPULATIONS

Nearly every troubling child suffers constantly from the tension of his muscles. If you go around a room of delinquent teens gently rubbing neck and shoulder muscles you will be astonished at the amount of pain, the fear of contact, the ejaculations of "Hey, what are you trying to do to me—Ouch!" As a relationship with a child is established physical manipulations should be accelerated.

With little kids a tickle session is often enough, with particular attention being paid to pressure on the middle of the long muscles of the back, the inner muscles of the thigh, and the muscles between chest and shoulders. The sessions can be great fun and with small children should not be pushed past one or two "ouch, that hurts."

With adolescents and adults a more formal session can be initiated beginning with light and pleasurable (if possible) back rubs, massaging all the great muscles in the limbs, and brisk rubs. If the facilities include steam rooms, saunas, whirlpool baths, etc., these can be integrated.

At some point the teacher or aide should begin to rub, squeeze and push slowly but vigorously in the muscles of the back and neck, subsequently moving to other areas. Each individual will display characteristic areas of severe pain. As these areas are addressed a great deal of emotion can be produced. The pupil can be told simply to let himself go and do anything, say anything, shout, cry or whatever. They usually will do so without being told, and the acceptance can readily be demonstrated. Telling first accelerates the process and the only advantage in not telling is to reassure the technician that she is not suggesting emotions where none exist.

There are a number of schools of "therapy" that will be horrified by these directions and will warn of all sorts of dire results. We have by now taught hundreds of children and adults a more easy awareness of their own flesh, emotions and the means of expressing such emotions through these tactics without any symptom substitution, or other harm. We have never had a worker hurt although a few sets of glasses have been broken (best to leave them off).

Nearly every person will show great pain if the muscles are pressed high in the neck, the muscles at the hinge of the jaw, the muscles directly over the shoulder blade about an inch outward from where it slopes down to the spine, the long muscles in the back at about two inches above the bottom of the shoulder blade, the muscles at the front of the shoulder joining it to the chest, the muscles at the top of the forearm about an inch down from the hinge pressing along the blade of the bone, the center of the ball of the thumb, the inner thighs, the upper center of the calf just below the hinge, the center of the ball of the great toe just above the arch. Nearly everyone, and certainly every troubled child, will experience a great deal of pain in other parts of the body. This pain will almost invariably be associated with a great deal of emotion.

A session ought normally to begin with easy massaging of the back then moving to the rest of the body. Before moving to a more vigorous manipulation go very gently, with just the tips of the fingers over the face, neck and upper body. Let the pupil focus for a while on how he is breathing. Then start again from the back, with particular emphasis on the long muscles and the pain area in the center. Address any knots, or pain areas, quite vigorously. The idea is to produce emotion and release the tension, not sneak up on it. You will find that general muscle relaxation is produced much more quickly by a vigorous assault. Sessions should be brief and slowly involve more areas of the body. Always pursue those areas which seem to be resisting, pulling away, or painful. We assume, of course, in all of our technical recommendations that a thorough medical inventory has been made of any student. The aide or teacher can report or discuss any abnormality with the physician and assist him in looking further. It is important to note that this is not a medical technique, is not designed to cure anything. It is a means of refocusing attention, rebuilding feedback, and reteaching the pupil how to control his own flesh. There is nothing mysterious or super powerful about it.

I have often been questioned about the brevity of these instructions. Experience has shown that the best way for a technician to develop competence with this routine is by self-instruction interacting with living pupils whose consequent actions and feelings are readily accessible to the worker. I do not believe in specialists being brought in for physical "therapy," occupational "therapy" or all the other pseudo medical specialities. Let the worker join the consequences with the pupil and a greater learning will be achieved. As far as this handbook is concerned the terms teacher, aide, therapist, worker, technician, engineer, etc., are all interchangeable. Such terms are usefully used only for administrative purposes.

An alert teacher will notice that troubled children cannot breathe. Their breathing—and that of many if not most Americans—

is thoroughly artificial. It is shallow, locked up into the chest with practically no chest movements and no abdominal movement at all. Observe a baby.

It will be helpful to use routines like HOLD YOUR BREATH. While lying down the children take as deep a breath as possible and hold it, then blow it all out at once. By pushing at the diaphragm, holding the chest, pushing down flatly with the palm against the chest, or, in the case of teens and adults, actually kneeling or sitting on the chest, the pupil can be sensitized to the possibility of abdominal breathing. They tend to get dizzy at first because they are not used to a lot of oxygen. Or just do TURN ON TO AIR in the class or during the manipulative sessions. Or have the kids blow up balloons, paper bags or air toys. Have them breathe in and out of a bladder or paper bag five or six times very rapidly. Have sessions of PANT LIKE A DOG. Show them how by placing your hand on your tummy and exaggeratedly moving it. All this will take a great deal of time. The characteristic style of clenching breath is the chief anxiety mechanism of many troubled individuals.

Of course, there are many people who over-breathe when they are anxious. It is likely that the shallow breathing clench is a reaction to the unpleasant effects of over-breathing (dizziness and general body discomfort—strong anxiety). This does not mean that deep breathing is bad. As long as the speed of deep breathing is consistent with the body's need for oxygen—which will depend on the amount of exertion—deep breathing will be comfortable and relaxing. If a person is inclined to over-breathe and so becomes anxious, jumpy, and worried by his body reactions, simple means can correct the vicious cycle (overbreathing/discomfort/overbreathing). A brown paper bag can be breathed into so that it expands and contracts for about three minutes with good effect. The person can be asked to sing or whistle, since both regulate breathing well. The exercises for breathing clench also work for over-breathing.

Pairing attention/relaxation/awareness routines with strenuous physical action will tend to break up the breathing clench. Drills and verbal/rational attention-forcing devices or discussion of breathing are not very useful. Many singers, dancers and others who have had a great deal of directive training, achieving a cortical control of vegetative functions, find that their anxieties, fears, and irrational liabilities are more tightly driven by the brain. This is not what we want.

PERCEPTUAL REEDUCATION

Every school should have accessible a whole range of illusions, distorted rooms and other materials that teach perceptual reorganization in nonverbal and overwhelming sensory presentations. An Ames room large enough for children to walk in is extremely useful. (This is the room that looks absolutely rectangular, but when a child stands in one corner he looks gigantic while an adult in the other corner looks tiny.) Other structures should be available which by their very nature force the pupil's eye to work in a novel fashion—buildings and rooms which are round, triangular, irregular or otherwise unusual.

It will be the very exceptional school system that has such resources, and few teachers will be blessed with an administration that understands how a woods ramble and run provides more contact with more perceptual retraining devices than a whole host of publishing houses.

It will likely be up to the teacher to fill her room with as many geometric forms, solid and plane, as possible. If the teacher can get away with having barriers of all kinds and shapes over or through which the children have to climb to move about the room, all the better. At the very least, teachers can usually get permission to make a huge construct outdoors in which the children can crawl, climb or walk as they create it, and enjoy it after the building.

More readily accessible illusions are the Ames Window and the Neckar Cube and Star. It is amazing how often children and adults are willing to look at these illusions. The Ames Window* is a trapezoidal window that viewed from afar at an angle appears rectangular.

*Appendix IV
(*Ames Room Illusion*)

If the window is rotated it appears not to be rotating but to be oscillating, going back and forth. If a pipe cleaner is fixed through one of the open panes of the window so that it extends past another pane, the eye suddenly sees the wire going completely around in the rotation, and the brain has to "see" that it goes through the solid window which is merely going back and forth and not all the way around. The Neckar Cube and the Star are wire forms which suddenly seem to reverse even though they are going in one direction only.

One of the best and most exciting visual illusions is given by the Ames distorted room.* An advantage of this device is that the room can be built in large enough proportions (say in a box 7' x 8' x 7') so that all sorts of things from the child's own real environment can be distorted with it. The room is radically distorted and when looked at from a particular observation point, is quite rectangular and symmetrical. If an object or person is viewed in the room or through one of the windows in the rear wall, the size of that object or person is radically distorted or altered to conform to the characteristics of the room. In this way, a child can exaggerate the size of a friend or a toy car; and make an enemy or his teacher appear very small.

The chief enjoyment of these tactics is that you can be pretty sure that no matter how badly this child has been taught before, he hasn't had this kind of experience. And he will see the illusion even if it takes some time. If he absolutely can't or takes an unusually long time, you had best call for that eye examination. Why push him into new failures just because you are asking him to walk when he doesn't own workable legs? The child has to learn. And he enjoys it. It's great fun to watch the "aha" phenomenon with each child or the whole class.

Simple paper and pencil illusions, or photo or printed illusions are widely accessible and children love them. What is more important, they learn from them to strengthen their perceptual organizing skills and begin to adopt a different set toward learning.

---

*See Appendix IV
(*Rotating Illusion*)
(*Ames Room Illusion*)

In general we find the drills commercially available for perceptual training are not only overpriced but make the fatal mistake of ignoring the fact that the perceptually limited child is usually a victim of overtraining and exacerbated anxiety. The training routines fall into the trap already baited by years of overanxious and controlling parents and teachers. I've never seen much point in putting a child on a little balance beam, or a balance disc when you could have them walk on post tops, or fences, or run through woods and climb fallen trees and slide into gullies. If we must have artificial equipment then it ought to be made attractive, adventurous and alive. A balance log three or six feet in the air begins to have some organic enjoyment and purpose in it. It can be made perfectly safe while enjoyable. In every way the drill approach should be avoided.

There doesn't seem to be much point in having children match up colored forms, or painfully copy forms with constant correction by teacher when by waiting a bit he'll be able to do it anyway. There are literally billions of environments and experiences that can be shaped to put the child through these skill needs without creating antagonism to authority or boredom with the drill.

There are now many nonverbal techniques for instruction, particularly in math, on the market. These techniques are also profoundly useful for perceptual sophistication. The Master Cube through which blind children learn algebra is equally useful for children who can see, both for learning algebra and for forcing eye/hand movements and explorations in new ways. Cuisenaire rods and other manipulanda supplied by the manufacturer of the rods are certainly useful. Blocks, geometric forms, free forms, pillow forms and toys, and other artifacts and solids are not merely toys, or academic aids. They are first line learning experiences that in the child's interaction with them force new data, new organization and structure, new skills into existence.

This is, by the way, no less true for the adolescent or the adult than for the elementary pupil. We have had 16-17 year old kids play all night long with one inch cube versions of the Cuisenaire rods; creating block houses, designs and other artifacts. We frequently regress the teen-age student all the way to kindergarten to reintroduce reading, writing, and calculating as well as perceptual skills within a framework of excited learning, usefulness and fun. Of course, sometimes we do this by telling them we are teaching them how to teach younger kids.

EMOTIONAL PERCEPTION

Specific routines to train more accurate emotional perceptions are frequently useful.

LIKE/DISLIKE

GENERAL DIRECTIONS: For about five minutes look around the room focusing on objects, and parts of objects. To each separate thing say "I am looking at this and I like it;" or "I don't like it;" "I *really* like it;" or "Ugh, that's disgusting."

Direct your children in doing this. Have them make up lists of things they like or dislike. Have them specify either to themselves or on paper or a tape what exactly it is they like or dislike. Do not be judgmental about their likes or dislikes. Make the game as enthusiastic as possible, or allow it to be silent and talking to yourself. Always indicate that their tapes and papers are their property. They can share them with others and with you if they wish. But they "are as private as the inside of your head. You can talk the inside out if you want, but if you don't, it can stay inside."

Remember you are not an analyst, you are not researching subtle nuances; you are teaching responsibility, attentiveness and contact. There is nothing particularly useful or illuminating about writing out or taping except as a bridge for the student. If the student has big blocks against writing, it is harmful to insist on writing. You must do everything possible to indicate that this is not like ordinary school work. There are going to be no marks or exams, which only apply to work that is examined and graded. You can even have them deposit the work in a box marked "secret" or "incinerator" to help loosen up the production jam.

FEELING TALK

GENERAL DIRECTIONS: For about five minutes think about things that you like, tastes, colors, shapes, houses, people, situations, experiences. Describe them to yourself as feelingly as possible. Inventory all your feelings and describe them. Put a value judgment on everything. "My stomach feels a bit tight and I don't like it." "My arms feel ready to work and I do like it." "I feel very rested and that's nice." "My head feels a bit stuffy and . . . " Work on things you do and don't like. Describe them as luridly and feelingly as you can. Play COMPLIMENT. How many nice good things can you think to say about someone else? Play CRITICIZE. How many nasty unliking things can you think up about someone or something you don't like?

This kind of exercise can be given as an assignment for broader use. "Try to compliment everyone you talk to today. Don't just describe the nice thing, but tell the person how nice you *feel* about it. Is there someone you really like? Tell them."

"Describe to someone else every nice thing that happens today. Try to do it as it happens. Is the food good? Say so. Is the air particularly fine? Say so. Do you like a sound, a particular arrangement of houses, or bushes? Say so."

Then try the reverse.

Try as much feeling-talk exercise as you can encourage. Support all talk about feelings and personal judgments, push further judgment—if a child likes a painting, what parts particularly? If he dislikes a sound, what does it do? What parts?

Separate feeling from evaluation.

Try to maintain a distinction between *feeling* and *evaluation*. For instance, "I feel he doesn't like me" is not a feeling but an evaluation. You might respond with "Where do you feel that?" or "You *believe* he doesn't like you." When carrying out routines in which you are encouraging a lot of personal feeling and evaluation these corrections should be made by gentle questioning or by rephrasing without too much directiveness. When routines are for training objectivity (see FAIR WITNESS below) then be as directive as you can: "I feel he is going to come;" "I feel like the test is going to be hard;" "I feel she cares." These are examples of predictions, opinions, beliefs, evaluations.

Even "I feel sad" is not sufficiently concrete and detailed. "I feel heavy in my eyes, my mouth feels dry, my back hurts, my head is light" are examples of direct feeling. Each feeling should be pushed for detail. "My back hurts" should be responded to with "Where does your back hurt?" and "How does that hurt feel to you?"

In a similar way a report that "She made me mad" should be pushed for correction to "I made myself mad because she did such and such." "I am sad because he took my favorite flowers out of the garden" not "He made me sad." "I am sad now" is not a complete description—inventorying all the feelings underlying the evaluative report of sadness is necessary.

REPORT, REPORT

Have the child describe something that just happened. It is preferable to have the first reporting about something which you saw and was fun and happy, so you can push for more detail, greater accuracy and more personalizing.

If a crisis occurs in the classroom, try to remove the most active or culpable person and immediately push for an accurate, detailed and personalized report. If it is a REPORT and REPORTS have already been made a part of the school routine, this will be greatly facilitated and the sense of punishment greatly reduced. You will be amazed at how remote something that just occurred can become. It is important that you very directly push for great detail, told in the first person. You should insist on feeling talk and concretization. Rejection is best given by repeated questioning rather than "You know that's not so." Merely repeating the evasion often moves things along, but don't be afraid to be blunt and corrective.

2 the tongue is a mighty member

THE TEACHER'S JOB is primarily a verbal job. Ideally the kind of physical learning and sophistication that a child needs to develop is given through organic structures, unselfconscious customs, and spontaneous activity in the structure of the class and culture. The re-educator has to do a great deal of more simply structured routine in these areas but her primary job is still verbal. It is almost always a breakdown of the smooth interaction between the verbal and motor system, with a failure of the verbal system, that is at the root of the failing child's problems.

The teacher must keep in mind that this kid is failing at tasks remarkably simpler than tasks he has already accomplished. Adding two and two is hardly as sophisticated as hitting a baseball. It is infinitely easier to learn to read and write than to listen and speak. If the child is failing it is because failing works for him.

The failing child has been taught to fail. It is up to you to create a learning excitement that recaptures skills he had when he learned to bring food to his mouth, to walk and to talk. The jobs he has now are much simpler.

The evidence is overwhelming that if you can teach this child to read with fluency, all his other problems, social and intellectual, will collapse. Fewer than ten per cent of all failing individuals (including social and intellectual failure) were fluent readers. Teaching children to read is the most powerful therapeutic intervention that can be made.

I
INTEGRATING PERCEPTION,
MOTOR COMMUNICATION AND WORDS

Many of the psychokinetic routines are preparation for the task of integrating the motor and verbal systems. When a class is at ease with the teacher a whole series of *Direct Contact* lessons should begin.

Play a piece of classical music to a quiet class. Do not discuss the music. Simply say "I am going to play a piece of music that many people think is beautiful. I want you to listen to it. I want you to listen to all of it as it goes along. If you want to move quietly you may."

Play the piece of music and then ask the children to talk, or write, or talk to the tape about what they heard. Do not suggest analyses. Let them come out of the children. Push by asking for more, for contrasts, for opposites, for levels, for relationships.

Put a painting in front of the class. Simply tell them "This is a painting many people think is beautiful. I want you to look at it, really look at it, for a few minutes." Then ask the children to describe, talking, writing, or taping, even sketching, what they saw. Compare it to a photo on the same easel.

Put a group of colored textiles or other textured materials on an easel in front of the class. Ask them merely to look at them, to look at them all the way, to try to get themselves inside the texture just by looking through their eyes. Then ask the children to describe what they saw. Push.

Play a recording of a poet reading. Don't try to plan down to the child. Put on a good poem. Try Dylan Thomas for the sonority of his voice. Do not explain or analyze. Ask the children to describe what they heard both for the sense impression and the content, but don't you differentiate. Just push.

Bring into class a collection of rocks. Have the children feel them. Touch them to all parts of the body. Taste them. Describe. Push.

Bring into class a collection of vases, bottles, and other glass containers. Look. Touch. Put water in and tap with a tiny metal hammer. Listen. Pour the water out. Listen. Take your time. Then have the children describe. You push.

Bring into class a bunch of big boxes, barrels, etc. Have the class crawl in, sit, stand, lie inside. Describe.

Blankets and cloths big enough to cover.

Darken the room and bring lights.

Slides and distorted slides.

Projected kaleidoscopes, strobe lamps. Posters.

Dough, clay, mud, oil, bread, sand, on the fingers.

Smells.

Tastes.

The important principle is to bring new experiences, or present old experiences from a new angle. Don't wall them in with words by talking about the experience, analyzing, or introducing. Encourage the children to talk, talk, talk, describe, describe, write, write, write after the experience. Don't grade the productions. What you are trying to teach is responsiveness, transaction with the environment, observation, analysis, reportage. Accuracy, style and grammar will come. Very quickly too.

THE CREATIVE USE OF CREATIVITY

It is very hard for children taught in American schools to escape the idea that they are being evaluated. It is awfully hard for them to try to do something on their own rather than trying to please you— the teacher. If the child merely pleases you, all you've done is grease your little ego without doing your job. What you are after is the disciplined use of skills he probably already has. You want the skill to be used exhuberantly toward the child's own ends. What good is it going to do him if he's still exercising his skills to please you when he ought to be solving real problems years later?

We have to invent ways of breaking up the pupil's failure experience, and his "what-does-teacher-want-now" set. So we've got to get him to write and talk about things he doesn't usually have in school, things that are funny or interesting because they are of immediate use to him. All such materials are full of data and skills that will be of use twenty years from now.

"Write about ghosts."

"Write about family fights."

"Write about the thing you like best in the world."

"Write down who should die."

"Write about your enemies."

"Write about the things and people you love most."

"Write about pirates, killers, dangerous beasts."

"Write about cars."

"Write about being married."

"Write about the thing you would most like to blow up."

"Write about someone who should be sick."

"What would you do if the sirens blew and the radio said we had fifteen minutes until the atomic bombs fell?"

"Think about how things might be if they were exactly the opposite of what they are now? What would you do if you were your dad, and he was you?"

"How would a backward day be?"

"How many things can you think of that are opposites?"

"What are the nastiest things you know?"

The important principles here are that children spontaneously talk about love, hate, violence, death, wrong things, nasty things, forbidden things. It is important that reporting, closely observing, analyzing, writing, talking, and reading be made useful to them. These stories will not usefully be graded. If the child begins to produce and produce, he will also increasingly approximate the norm of the spoken and written communications he absorbs around him. What you are teaching is success at words. Grammar is an intuitive tool.

There are a host of creativity games available.

Using physical objects, instruct the children to arrange them in any fashion they like. Then rearrange. Then arrange again. "How many titles can you make for what you just made?" "How many things can you think it might be?"

Write or tell stories about pictures, or groups of objects. Tell another story. Another. "What's the shortest story you can tell about it?"

Have each child give everyone in the room a nickname. "Make a list of names as if someone were going to give you ten dogs; cats, horses, whales, dodos, kangaroos, anything."

The teacher can even use the child's authoritarianism which blocks creativity to advantage in shaping creativity into the child. If the child is particularly prone to seeing what the teacher wants now, and cannot find novel or varied associations in games being played, the group can be asked to take turns giving verbal or gutteral associations to any stimulus word. The teacher could then compliment each increasingly novel or non-sensible association, thus shaping the group movement toward novelty. This will be easier with simple, single sounds than with complex tasks. A slight alteration of the game asks for novel ways of using the same ideas or words, or for novel combinations of simple words and ideas.

Use clay, play dough, sand, think sticks, construction sets, blocks, and finger paints. Have the children talk and write about what they made. Don't think that adults or adolescents can't benefit from these materials and procedures.

"How many different ways can you put together a person?"

Use blocks, beads, pillows, jigsaw cutouts, balls, rings, etc. Give each child a try at many different things. "Make people as many different ways as you can."

"Can you draw a person just with sticks? Now try just with circles. How about ovals? How about squares? Rectangles? Triangles? Now make a person using something altogether new."

"Can you use a car for ten different things? How many different uses can be devised for how many different artifacts?"

Use books of riddles, puzzles, mazes. (Dover Press has several)

Make up whole lists of three dimensional puzzles for your children. For example: Lay out six matches and ask them to make four equal triangles with them. The clue is "Why does it have to be flat?"

Use verbal puzzles and logic problems for fun.

"An explorer went to an island on which there were two tribes. One tribe was very peaceful and helpful and always, but always tells the truth. The other tribe just could not tell the truth ever, and as you might expect, they always killed strangers as soon as they could. Well, the explorer got up on the beach of the island and saw two natives coming. He shouted to the first "What tribe do you belong to?" But the native's answer was obscured by a falling tree. By this time the second fellow was closer so the explorer asked him "What did he say he was?" This chap says "Why he said he was a Liar Tribe." Whereupon Mr. Explorer hauls out his pistol and shoots one of the natives. He shot the right one. And he did have enough evidence. Which one? Why?

"A train is going 100 miles an hour down a track. As it passes an oak tree a man shoots off a crossbow from the back platform. This crossbow shoots an arrow that goes 100 yards and averages 100 miles an hour. He shoots it straight out the back along the tracks. Where, in relation to the oak tree, does the arrow land?" (As you go along with this puzzle draw a box car 100 yards long and have the crossbow shoot from one end to another both in the direction the train is going, and back. Then when the train isn't moving, take it back out of the boxcar to the platform.)

"When a man jumps out of an airplane he accelerates up to about 120 miles per hour. Then he falls at a steady rate buoyed up by the air until he abruptly stops. If he opens a parachute he'll slow down to a speed that depends on the size of the canopy and weight. Once he reaches that speed he'll stay at a constant speed until he hits the ground. If he had a compressed helium container and a balloon he would slow down, maybe stop, and even start accelerating upwards until he got high enough for the pressures to balance; then he'd float. What I want to know is when that fellow has stopped accelerating down, opens his parachute and stops slowing down and is falling at a steady rate, which force is stronger—the one pulling him down or the one pushing him up?" (As you give this one ask what would happen if the opposite one were stronger. Then the opposite.) It is hard to get, but the answer is that unless it's accelerating, both forces are equal even though it's whizzing along. You can also try by making the thing fall to the airless moon. Or ask them to contemplate two space ships passing in the void. What does one know about the other if it's just mooching along but at 1, then 2, then 3, then 4 miles an hour as he watches for four minutes.

The point of such problems is that if they are given in a lively way they are unlike puzzles and problems in the past. With patience and individual work almost every child over ten can solve them, and will experience a good insight as a result. The alert teacher will reward the solution with enthusiasm, no matter how long it takes. And it will be a real solution.

When you want to come closer to ordinary classwork there are nice little enigmas like:

"Suppose two companies offered you jobs. You were going to be in a situation in which you couldn't quit for ten years or so—maybe working on Venus. As a result, you wanted to be sure to get the best pay situation since everything else between the companies seemed absolutely equal. One company offered you $10,000 a year with raises of $1,000 starting in the second year and paid at the end of every year thereafter. The other company offered you $10,000 a year and would pay you $500 raises each year, but it would start after the first six months and be paid at the end of each six months ($250 each six months). Which job would you take?"

You'll have to write this one down to believe it. It makes a big impression on students, and there are many such problems. If teens are going to be impressed with the fun and usefulness of calculation it might as well be with striking problems like this rather than dull exercises. Time enough to practice calculation when you have to work in a store, build something, repair cars and engines or other work—almost all of which requires numbers. Could you tell by sight if a nut takes a 7/16 or a half inch wrench? Many of your failing boys can.

MATERIALS THAT TEACH

Cuisenaire rods, master cubes and other nonverbal instructional devices are useful not only for their direct functions—teaching math or algebra, or for use in perceptual retraining—but can also be used as unique materials for developing expression, reportage, and writing. The important thing to remember is that children have been asked to write about all kinds of things that have no real interest to them. They can directly perceive and manipulate these objects and can tell you a great deal about them. Whatever they write will be accurate, if not imaginative. Most delinquent youngsters will be very taciturn and boringly ordinary in their productions. Younger children referred for class difficulty, however, will much more likely be quite creative in their writing about such arrangements of materials. Highly creative children of low tested intelligence are those most likely to have a rough time in the normal classroom—even more so than children of both low tested intelligence and low creativity.

The proper job of a child is to play and play and play. There is no play that does not teach, and no experience out of which a child cannot learn. With remedial problems the critical awareness the teacher needs to act upon is that these kids have been sadly insulated from their perceptions and skills. Therefore they need to have situations provided in which their play can be enriched with artifacts or natural forms. If the child thinks that the play is a Learning Experience you might as well go back to *Dick and Jane.*

COORDINATION, CONTACT AND BALANCE

All of the psychokinetic routines are devised to enhance coordination, awareness and balance. Wherever these routines have been established, without any other educational intervention, academic achievement has gone up dramatically. *They are methods of reading instruction and of intellectual instruction.*

Coordination training can be focused down to more specific routines, particularly for children who resist more organic exercises. Daily practice on balance fences and beams—still preferably large enough and high enough to improve interest and motivation, and other physical routines requiring balance and coordination are useful, particularly if the teacher or aide goes through the same routines. Dodge runs (running through a course broken up with panels or tires or other obstacles), running along tops of fence posts set for the size of the child, confidence courses, rope climbs, etc., are all helptul if vigorously done.

A hand tremor test ought to be part of the routine of every school. This simple device can be made in any rudimentary electronic shop. A sheet of thin aluminum has a number of holes bored in it ranging down from one inch. A long narrow slot is also cut into it as is a long narrow vee. A metal stylus is wired to one side of a bell or buzzer and the metal is wired to the other so that touching the metal with the stylus closes the circuit and causes the buzzer to sound. A tremulous person is going to have difficulty in any stress situation. Control can be built up by short daily sessions of practice in holding the stylus in progressively smaller holes, running along the slot and down the vee without buzzing.

A rotary pursuit device can easily be made of an old phonograph turntable. A two inch hole is cut into the edge of the turntable and its sides painted with aluminum paint so that contact can be made. A metal stylus is wired to one side of a bell circuit and the other is wired to the paint leading from the hole in the turntable. The pupil tries to follow the hole with the stylus in it. If he does not keep it centered the bell rings. This can be great fun, and will be even more fun if the teacher secures prism lenses that distort vision 10 or 15 degrees to right or left or even crossing the eyes.

These sessions should be brief. The speed should never be increased until a slower speed is thoroughly mastered. The teacher should always praise and reward the performance.

A disc can be cut out of peg board and mounted on a nail against a wall so that it turns freely. It can then be spun by hand and golf tees pushed into the holes as it turns starting from the center out. The disc can be motorized, of course.

Suspend a ball from the ceiling by a cord and swing it. Follow it with one eye covered, then the other, then follow it with both eyes.

Prepare cards with six point size type (want ad size) read at arms length, then slowly bring in, reading all the way, until it blurs, then switch to calendar sized type on poster on the wall. Try with one eye, then the other, then both.

Read for five minutes with the book so close that the print blurs at first.

All of these exercises can be done for about three to five minutes three times a day and will produce immediate improvement.

Tell the kiddies to try to walk places with their heads straight ahead, seeing things out of the corners of their eyes. First one then the other, then both.

If you can buy a photo electric motion sensor you can play games of SURVEILLANCE which really see how long the child can sit quietly without making the sensor sound its alarm. Standing and holding a teaspoon of water for two minutes, or other steadiness

games are just as good. There are also motion sensors that are con-
nected to pneumatic cushions on which the child sits. If you can get a
system rigged up that makes static or other noises as the child wiggles
in his seat you can develop games in which the child builds in control
of movement and holding still. Making a sensor read out with wavey
lines on an oscilloscope screen is electronically quite easy. The kids
will love it.

II
REDUCING ABSTRACTION

Years of work with disturbing and failing youngsters have convinced us that, far from being unable to cope with abstraction, they
are practically incapable of dealing with the world around them and
their own internal feelings in a concrete, and specific way. We find
that routines for training directly the reduction of generalization and
abstraction are very helpful for emotional, behavioral and academic
skills.

FAIR WITNESS TRAINING. This is somewhat related to RE-
PORT, REPORT in that the teacher is highly directive, constantly
corrects and drives toward objectivity of description. A picture is
shown to the student and he is asked to describe the picture in great
detail, and as economically as possible. No deductions or speculations are permitted. For instance, if he is shown a picture of a basket
full of kittens and says "There are some kittens who have just had
their milk." The teacher says "Where is the milk?" The teacher keeps
pushing for more and more detail and rejects speculations and ab-
stractions by asking "Where?", "What kind?", "How do you know?"
A pretty fast pace is maintained throughout. This differs from RE-
PORT, REPORT in that value judgments and feelings of the person
toward the picture are not asked for and are vigorously excluded.
This can be done by correcting writing, but only with kids who have
very high verbal intelligence. It ought to be done individually or with
small groups only.

GENERALIZATION ABSTRACTION PROCEDURE (GAP). This routine involves 120 slides graded in a hierarchy from least to most general and abstract. On the slide are four choices describing the figure. The most concrete and economical is the correct choice. For instance, a figure of a coat hanger can be clearly a coat hanger and not just a hanger, or hook, or pants hanger. A table knife can be clearly not a butcher knife, not just a knife or a utensil. Some operators automate the presentation so that wrong answers get a buzz and right answers a ding dong or bell. We simply hold the slide until the right answer is produced and move on. A very rapid pace can be set and very young pupils will move quickly through the 120 slides.

FOREIGN ENGLISH. Nearly any English writing can be translated into the 800 or so words of Basic English. Difficult children will hate this, so it ought to be brought into a class rather late in your experiment with it. She can start by asking the kids to write something as simple as possible. Then introduce the idea of Basic English and give material to be translated. Ask for essays in Basic English only. See if the class can become fluent in Basic English by giving everyone 50 pennies and allowing them to fine each other for slips—use the money for a class party. Or let the winners keep it.

Difficult children can be induced to enjoy Basic English by giving them something pompously moralistic to translate; or first show them a translation of some pompous moralizing, then give them another to have a go at. Translating the ideas of politicians and educational philosophers is always great fun.

Problem children will enjoy Basic English more if it is first introduced by writing and talking in purposefully bad grammar. Accents and dialects and artificial grammars (say, write without any past tense, without any plurals, be mock angry at any lapse into mistaken correct grammar). Have them write, eliminating as many grammatical features as they can think of. Offer a prize for the most fractured piece of writing. Make up a new grammar. Reintroduce thee and thou. Talk about languages with rising and falling modes for addressing peers, inferiors and superiors. Examine codes and problems of communicating without an agreed code through someone you don't want to understand. Have one group of boys write a message in clear English and give it to the teacher. Then have the boys write it so that they don't think the girls will understand it but that another group of boys will. Give the message to the girls for five minutes, and then on to the other boys. If the girls get it, they win. Can the boys write the girls a message the teacher can't translate (and don't try too hard)? Talk about slang. Give a prize for the most unintelligible piece of slang. Have referees to determine if it really is language in currency.

Have the group write haiku. Start them with examples of these 17 syllable poems about anything. Have them do some for sharing first, then write their own, very privately.

CONDITIONED ACCELERATION OF RESPONSES BY RELIEF OF AVERSION (CARRA). We use CARRA with a simple electric stimulator. We tell the pupil that we are going to turn on a mild tingle and then increase it. We will turn it off when the pupil makes a new response to the category we are asking for. For example: "I want you to tell me something you might say to your mother when you wake up in the morning. Each time tell me something different."

When we get a response that is not a repetition we immediately turn the current off. It can be done without electric stimulation but no one seems to mind very much and it works a great deal more quickly. For many kids, switching on a red light seems to work just as well (inward kids who are quiet, with downcast eyes, and sullen kids mostly). For others, simply driving an answer with verbal encouragement and direction will work. The advantage of electric reinforcement is that it is simple, matter of fact, unavoidable, and does not require verbal skill on the part of the teacher or aide. Also we seem to build up a tolerance for electric stimulation which in general seems to correlate quite well with general stability in the nervous system. In addition, the conditioning model is more precise and we seem to get a spill-over of conditioning for anxiety relief and a sense of being in control of the anxiety-producing stimulus.

The routine goes only about five minutes and any category is stopped as soon as it becomes a bit sticky for the student to think of something new. We are not trying to punish the child or test him.

BASIC ENGLISH

OPERATIONS
100 ETC.

COME	WILL	TO	SUCH	WHY	LITTLE
GET	ABOUT	UNDER	THAT	AGAIN	MUCH
GIVE	ACROSS	UP	THIS	EVER	NOT
GO	AFTER	WITH	I	FAR	ONLY
KEEP	AGAINST	AS	HE	FORWARD	QUITE
LET	AMONG	FOR	YOU	HERE	SO
MAKE	AT	OF	WHO	NEAR	VERY
PUT	BEFORE	TILL	AND	NOW	TOMORROW
SEEM	BETWEEN	THAN	BECAUSE	OUT	YESTERDAY
TAKE	BY	A	BUT	STILL	NORTH
BE	DOWN	THE	OR	THEN	SOUTH
DO	FROM	ALL	IF	THERE	EAST
HAVE	IN	ANY	THROUGH	TOGETHER	WEST
SAY	OFF	EVERY	WHILE	WELL	PLEASE
SEE	ON	NO	HOW	ALMOST	YES
SEND	OVER	OTHER	WHEN	ENOUGH	
MAY	THROUGH	SOME	WHERE	EVEN	

THINGS
400 GENERAL

ACCOUNT	BUSINESS	DEATH	FATHER	IDEA	MAN	ORDER
ACT	BUTTER	DEBT	FEAR	IMPULSE	MANAGER	ORGANIZA
ADDITION	CANVAS	DECISION	FEELING	INCREASE	MARK	ORNAMENT
ADJUSTMENT	CARE	DEGREE	FICTION	INDUSTRY	MARKET	OWNER
ADVERTISEMENT	CAUSE	DESIGN	FIELD	INK	MASS	PAGE
AGREEMENT	CHALK	DESIRE	FIGHT	INSECT	MEAL	PAIN
AIR	CHANCE	DESTRUCTION	FIRE	INSTRUMENT	MEASURE	PAINT
AMOUNT	CHANGE	DETAIL	FLAME	INSURANCE	MEAT	PAPER
AMUSEMENT	CLOTH	DEVELOPMENT	FLIGHT	INTEREST	MEETING	PART
ANIMAL	COAL	DIGESTION	FLOWER	INVENTION	MEMORY	PASTE
ANSWER	COLOUR	DIRECTION	FOLD	IRON	METAL	PAYMENT
APPARATUS	COMFORT	DISCOVERY	FOOD	JELLY	MIDDLE	PEACE
APPROVAL	COMMITTEE	DISCUSSION	FORCE	JOIN	MILK	PERSON
ARGUMENT	COMPANY	DISEASE	FORM	JOURNEY	MIND	PLACE
ART	COMPARISON	DISGUST	FRIEND	JUDGE	MINE	PLANT
ATTACK	COMPETITION	DISTANCE	FRONT	JUMP	MINUTE	PLAY
ATTEMPT	CONDITION	DISTRIBUTION	FRUIT	KICK	MIST	PLEASURE
ATTENTION	CONNECTION	DIVISION	GLASS	KISS	MONEY	POINT
ATTRACTION	CONTROL	DOUBT	GOLD	KNOWLEDGE	MONTH	POISON
AUTHORITY	COOK	DRINK	GOVERNMENT	LAND	MORNING	POLISH
BACK	COPPER	DRIVING	GRAIN	LANGUAGE	MOTHER	PORTER
BALANCE	COPY	DUST	GRASS	LAUGH	MOTION	PORTER
BASE	CORK	EARTH	GRIP	LAW	MOUNTAIN	POSITION
BEHAVIOUR	COTTON	EDGE	GROUP	LEAD	MOVE	POWDER
BELIEF	COUGH	EDUCATION	GROWTH	LEARNING	MUSIC	POWER
BIRTH	COUNTRY	EFFECT	GUIDE	LEATHER	NAME	PRICE
BIT	COVER	END	HARBOUR	LETTER	NATION	PRINT
BITE	CRACK	ERROR	HARMONY	LEVEL	NEED	PRODUCE
BLOOD	CREDIT	EVENT	HATE	LIFT	NEWS	PROFIT
BLOW	CRIME	EXAMPLE	HEARING	LIGHT	NIGHT	PROPERTY
BODY	CRUSH	EXCHANGE	HEAT	LIMIT	NOISE	PROSE
BRASS	CRY	EXISTENCE	HELP	LINEN	NOTE	PROTEST
BREAD	CURRENT	EXPANSION	HISTORY	LIQUID	NUMBER	PULL
BREATH	CURVE	EXPERIENCE	HOLE	LIST	OBSERVATION	PUNISHME
BROTHER	DAMAGE	EXPERT	HOPE	LOOK	OFFER	PURPOSE
BUILDING	DANGER	FACT	HOUR	LOSS	OIL	PUSH
BURN	DAUGHTER	FALL	HUMOUR	LOVE	OPERATION	QUALITY
BURST	DAY	FAMILY	ICE	MACHINE	OPINION	QUESTION

THINGS

RAIN	ROLL	SHOCK	SONG	SUMMER	TRANSPORT	WEATHER
RANGE	ROOM	SIDE	SORT	SUPPORT	TRICK	WEEK
RATE	RUB	SIGN	SOUND	SURPRISE	TROUBLE	WEIGHT
RAY	RULE	SILK	SOUP	SWIM	TURN	WIND
REACTION	RUN	SILVER	SPACE	SYSTEM	TWIST	WINE
READING	SALT	SISTER	STAGE	TALK	UNIT	WINTER
REASON	SAND	SIZE	START	TASTE	USE	WOMAN
RECORD	SCALE	SKY	STATEMENT	TAX	VALUE	WOOD
REGRET	SICENCE	SLEEP	STEAM	TEACHING	VERSE	WOOL
RELATION	SEA	SLIP	STEEL	TENDENCY	VESSEL	WORD
RELIGION	SEAT	SLOPE	STEP	TEST	VIEW	WORK
REPRESENTATIVE	SECRETARY	SMASH	STITCH	THEORY	VOICE	WOUND
REQUEST	SELECTION	SMELL	STONE	THING	WALK	WRITING
RESPECT	SELF	SMILE	STOP	THOUGHT	WAR	YEAR
REST	SENSE	SMOKE	STORY	THUNDER	WASH	
REWARD	SERVANT	SNEEZE	STRETCH	TIME	WASTE	
RHYTHM	SEX	SNOW	STRUCTURE	TIN	WATER	
RICE	SHADE	SOAP	SUBSTANCE	TOP	WAVE	
RIVER	SHAKE	SOCIETY	SUGAR	TOUCH	WAX	
ROAD	SHAME	SON	SUGGESTION	TRADE	WAY	

200 Picturable

ANGLE	BRANCH	DOG	HAND	NECK	ROOF	STICK
ANT	BRICK	DOOR	HAT	NEEDLE	ROOT	STOCKING
APPLE	BRIDGE	DRAIN	HEAD	NERVE	SAIL	STOMACH
ARCH	BRUSH	DRAWER	HEART	NET	SCHOOL	STORE
ARM	BUCKET	DRESS	HOOK	NOSE	SCISSORS	STREET
ARMY	BULB	DROP	HORN	NUT	SCREW	SUN
BABY	BUTTON	EAR	HORSE	OFFICE	SEED	TABLE
BAG	CAKE	EGG	HOSPITAL	ORANGE	SHEEP	TAIL
BALL	CAMERA	ENGINE	HOUSE	OVEN	SHELF	THREAD
BAND	CARD	EYE	ISLAND	PARCEL	SHIP	THROAT
BASIN	CART	FACE	JEWEL	PEN	SHIRT	THUMB
BASKET	CARRIAGE	FARM	KETTLE	PENCIL	SHOE	TICKET
BATH	CAT	FEATHER	KEY	PICTURE	SKIN	TOE
BED	CHAIN	FINGER	KNEE	PIG	SKIRT	TONGUE
BEE	CHEESE	FISH	KNIFE	PIN	SNAKE	TOOTH
BELL	CHEST	FLAG	KNOT	PIPE	SOCK	TOWN
BERRY	CHIN	FLOOR	LEAF	PLANE	SPADE	TRAIN
BIRD	CHURCH	FLY	LEG	PLATE	SPONGE	TRAY
BLADE	CIRCLE	FOOT	LIBRARY	PLOUGH	SPOON	TREE
BOARD	CLOCK	FORK	LINE	POCKET	SPRING	TROUSERS
BOAT	CLOUD	FOWL	LIP	POT	SQUARE	UMBRELLA
BONE	COAT	FRAME	LOCK	POTATO	STAMP	WALL
BOOK	COLLAR	GARDEN	MAP	PRISON	STAR	WATCH
BOOT	COMB	GIRL	MATCH	PUMP	WINDOW	WHEEL
BOTTLE	CORD	GLOVE	MONKEY	RAIL	WING	WHIP
BOX	COW	GOAT	MOON	RAT	WIRE	WHISTLE
BOY	CUP	GUN	MOUTH	RECEIPT	WORM	
BRAIN	CURTAIN	HAIR	MUSCLE	RING	STATION	
BRAKE	CUSHION	HAMMER	NAIL	ROD	STEM	

QUALITIES
100 General   50 Opposites

ABLE	ELASTIC	KIND	PROBABLE	THICK	DEAD	OPPOSITE
ACID	ELECTRIC	LIKE	QUICK	TIGHT	DEAR	PUBLIC
ANGRY	EQUAL	LIVING	QUIET	TIRED	DELICATE	ROUGH
AUTOMATIC	FAT	LONG	READY	TRUE	DIFFERENT	SAD
BEAUTIFUL	FERTILE	MALE	RED	VIOLENT	DIRTY	SAFE
BLACK	FIRST	MARRIED	REGULAR	WAITING	DRY	SECRET
BOILING	FIXED	MATERIAL	RESPONSIBLE	WARM	FALSE	SHORT
BRIGHT	FLAT	MEDICAL	RIGHT	WET	FEEBLE	SHUT
BROKEN	FREE	MILITARY	ROUND	WIDE	FEMALE	SIMPLE
BROWN	FREQUENT	NATURAL	SAME	WISE	FOOLISH	SLOW
CHEAP	FULL	NECESSARY	SECOND	YELLOW	FUTURE	SMALL
CHIEF	GENERAL	NEW	SEPARATE	YOUNG	GREEN	SOFT
CHEMICAL	GOOD	NORMAL	SERIOUS	AWAKE	ILL	SOLID
CLEAN	GREAT	OPEN	SHARP	BAD	LAST	SPECIAL
CLEAR	GREY	PARALLEL	SMOOTH	BENT	LATE	STRANGE
COMMON	HANGING	PAST	STICKY	BITTER	LEFT	THIN
COMPLEX	HAPPY	PHYSICAL	STIFF	BLUE	LOOSE	WHITE
CONSCIOUS	HARD	POLITICAL	STRAIGHT	CERTAIN	LOUD	WRONG
CUT	HEALTHY	POOR	STRONG	COLD	LOW	
DEEP	HIGH	POSSIBLE	SUDDEN	COMPLETE	MIXED	
DEPENDENT	HOLLOW	PRESENT	SWEET	CRUEL	NARROW	
EARLY	IMPORTANT	PRIVATE	TALL	DARK	OLD	

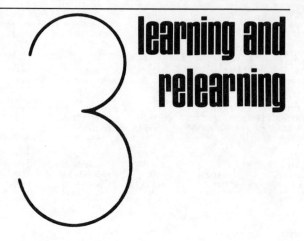

3 learning and relearning

THE EFFECTIVE USE OF PROGRAMMING. Programmed instruction has received an enormous amount of attention in the last several years. If everything is equal, programmed learning has no advantages over other kinds of learning. Its great initial successes came because controls and comparisons were made with the worst sort of conventional instruction. If vivid and attractive materials are provided and children are permitted to teach themselves, or each other, all of the advantages disappear. The most useful function of programmed materials is that they force writers to become economical and relevant.

One advantage of programmed instruction, particularly by machine, is that it enables the special teacher to break the conditioned transaction that troubled kids have in which learning has something to do with the fight against authority. Retarded children, in particular institutionalized retarded kids, seem to do much better with programmed instruction. They are the only population in which rewards for correct responses are quite a bit more effective than simple knowledge of correct results. This seems to be so because these kids have been trained to respond to adults around them rather than to learn. In addition, because of their intellectual weakness this kind of training takes root more seriously than in other kids. The opposite problem is true with difficult children. They tend to do exactly what the adults don't want them to do. Charles Slack has been having Puerto Rican janitors (preferably with little or no English) bring teaching machines into cells with young criminals. The janitor gets it across that the machine is supposed to teach the kids. He also gets it across that since it is the machine's job to *teach,* if the kid makes a mistake the machine will give him a dime for having wasted his time.

Nearly everyone rubs their eyes at this point. *The machine gives the student a dime if the student makes a mistake* because the machine has not done its job and taught him. These young criminals do not work to make mistakes or to make dimes. No one has to con these kids into the advantages of knowing. They do quite well for themselves if the social consequences and structures of the *teaching* process are changed. Many of these hoods work for hours at a time on the machines and graduate from jail to college.

I might insert here that our schools orient a student at an early stage with a comment "I don't care whether you work hard or not. I don't care if you want to help yourself or not. You are going to learn here if you want to or not, motivated or not. Our job is to teach you and we, by God, are going to teach you."

The important thing about good programmed material is that it makes it easier for the child to teach himself, or for the child to teach other children, by making the material we want the child to know more accessible, vivid and comprehensible.

Children are motor creatures. No mother needs to be told that they are almost always active. Their first "reasoning" and problem solving involves using large muscles. By the third year they are efficient computers. They can cross unknown rooms full of strange people and objects without difficulty. This is a computing task. Engineers call the kind of computing that babies do "analog" computation. An everyday example of an analog computer is the gas pedal on a car.

Instead of dialing or punching a code "45 miles an hour," you push a pedal a certain distance that is translated into the car's speed at 45 miles an hour. Your foot is part of a feedback link to maintain the speed. Most people don't even think about it. Children operate all the time by such methods. They don't need logic or words or numbers to carry out the really enormous number of tasks they have learned since birth. They make associations, read signs and interpret much data—from mother's frown to how much chocolate is left in a pan.

Children are visual creatures. The average *adult* receives more than three quarters of his useful information about the world through his eyes. The child's world is even more visual. Children are used to making some kind of useful order out of unstructured "realities." They can see a butterfly against a background of flowers (often when an adult cannot). They can recognize a tiny formal design on a dress and associate it with its "real" counterpart. They can draw apparently shapeless figures and recognize them much later as "cow," "Mommy" or whatever it was they thought they were drawing at first.

Children do not "absorb" information. What they do is much closer to *grab*. They actually reach out and take hold of information. This means that the vividness of the things we want them to learn must be strong. Psychologists call a related process "imprinting." The initial imprint is very important. We recognize this in the thoughtfulness and planning that goes into a supermarket or an advertisement. Vividly presented material is grasped immediately by the interested child. Young children are almost always interested in any information that is intelligible to them. If they have to be motivated to learn we know that something has already gone wrong.

Children remember through a process known to computer engineers as "sparse exploratory scanning." This simply means that tiny, or sparse, cues can be used to trigger a complicated series of events stored in the brain. The cue is found by scanning, or skimming—skipping from cue to cue. Many adults remember in a very different fashion. They are like librarians looking from category to category—indexing. This kind of remembering is used particularly for verbal information and is used by professional and scholarly people more than by workers and artists. Teachers are ordinarily very verbal, being educated middle class people who almost always retrieve information by indexing. Much of their trouble with children is that they think in different ways.

Neither indexers nor scanners are helped a great deal by repetition. It is far more useful to spend time trying to recall something you've just read than to read it repeatedly. It is even more useful to *use* the information—not repeat it, but use it.

Deprived children are almost always more motor (even though they may be very quiet, their quiet is not thoughtful), more visual and more dependent on vividness of imprint than middle class children. They reason almost entirely through physical, motor analogs. Their memories rely almost entirely on sparse exploratory scanning. They seldom have any orderly patterns of behavior at all—certainly their mental or logical patterns are not precise. Slum cultures are characterized by a high background noise level that obscures communication of information about the external world. Words are used, but they are almost always expressions of emotional tone.

In many ways the slum child is like the developmentally slow child, and for many of the same reasons. Experiences simply have not or do not impinge on the child. Troubling youngsters experience, respond, communicate, remember and learn in almost the same fashion. Because of the very high arousal (anxiety, hunger for contact, simple hunger, confusion, etc., all cause arousal that blocks perception) even the very wealthy failing child does not experience the rightness of his environment and so cannot learn.

GOOD INSTRUCTIONAL MATERIAL is big. If the paper or book is not physically big, then the letters and symbols in it should be. Children feel more at home with a big book than with a small one, but the book shouldn't be too thick. In fact, good instructional material can be presented a page at a time.

Work spaces and blank space should be large, not regular and not confined. Blanks to fill in are usually confining and confusing.

Good instructional material uses simple, vivid, uncluttered symbols. Richness of detail in toys and symbols inhibit fantasy and creative projections. Toys and symbols should be vivid, but simple. Lines should be uncluttered. In this case, vivid does not necessarily mean bright and colorful, but clear, with dramatic lines.

The symbols in materials to be widely used should be nearly culture free. They should be drawn from the universal symbolic treasure chest common to all children. They should be useable with urban, rural, wealthy, poor, verbal in all degrees, bright or dull children. Thoughtfulness is needed here. In some of our material we tried to build association for the letter "p" with "Policeman's Pistol," and we found that slum children did not use the words policeman or pistol. Cop and gun were the only vivid words for these realities.

Lettering should be informal and loose. Letters and symbols should not be exactly alike. Kids don't live in a uniform world. The uniformity of printing actually inhibits learning to read and write. Children learn much more quickly from teachers who print out words for them than from printed primers.

No attempt should be made to regularize the child's production of the symbols or figures. Disadvantaged and non-English speaking children should never have *any* book given to them as their first drawing or writing experience. They should be given at least several days of nothing but free expression on similar sized paper or with chalk at a board. Rolling out newsprint on the floor and letting the children draw all over it will help to bring them to more controlled work. Good instructional materials provide a great deal of room for "play." And a good teacher doesn't try to direct that play back to her idea of what is related to the material.

One simple, vivid idea or datum should be introduced on a page. Whether the level of instruction is elementary or advanced the concept should be boiled down to bare essentials and presented as baldly as possible. This is really the great advantage of programming. It forces a discipline on the teacher to present material in the terse, matter-of-fact way preferred by children. The child is perfectly competent to elaborate. Having learned to enjoy it, reading then becomes a fleshing out of the bones structured in class. Reading will then be a part of play, an activity essentially free of authority conflict.

The material should be presented quickly, brusquely, in a matter-of-fact fashion. Correct responses can be recognized with a simple "That's Good," "Very Good" or "OK." Incorrect responses should always be ignored. If the teacher is presenting the material, the time pace should be rapid and, within the subsections of the material, should move ahead without waiting for correct responses. The child can set the pace of forward movement from subsection to subsection, but the daily presentation of material should take just about the same time. The pace should be exciting, fast and noisy.

There is absolutely no evidence to support the superstition that the material should progress step by step in some logical framework. Think for a moment of some skill you have learned. Was it grasped by someone else's logic or your own?

A good teacher will make all of her exams occasions for learning in the model of programmed materials.

Many years ago Pressey came out with what amounted to being the first teaching machine, with cards for testing that gave immediate knowledge of results and consequent learning.

The Pressey card had questions prepared on index-cards with multiple choice answers and either "c" or "x" typed next to the answer. The "c" and "x" were covered with pencil graphite so that all the students had to do was erase until he got the right answer. It was easy to tell how often he had to erase, so a daily score of his immediate learning could be kept. The student got an immediate objectification of how much he knew and learned the right answer immediately.

Any professional teacher can prepare these materials with a minimum of effort.

SENTENCE COMPLETION. We have found that slum kids love sentence completion tasks. Many of our slum classes have a great deal of "homework" (and discipline is maintained by threatening not to give the homework). Since we know the homes are usually impossible for homework—and since those with well motivated and anxious parents can be truthfully informed "I did it at school"—the homework is given for the last period before 3 o'clock. This homework consists of sentence completions prepared the night before on ditto sheets. The sentences are related to the ongoing experiences in the class and are not sentence completion tests. That is, they are not of the nature of "Columbus discovered America in ----------." They are on the order of "Juan shot a spitball at Mary and she ------------." Retarded and other limited children have much the same cognitive experiences and liabilities as slum children and the same tactics are useful. These kids are not used to thinking in completed and extended rational statements. They are more likely to respond to signs than symbols. The use of sentence completion will fit easily into the programmed structure.

ORGANIC READING is the term coined by Sylvia Ashton Warner for the instructional methods described in her marvelous book, *Teacher*.

The basic idea of organic instruction is that teaching ought to begin as close to the organic, living world of the child as possible. If, for reasons external to the child, it progresses away from that world, then it ought to do it by tiny steps, each related back to the vital ongoing concerns of the child.

In the organic primary class, reading is ritualized into a rhythm of class day that alternates outgoing and vigorous periods with quiet and inward periods. Reading is an active, noisy, happy affair. It is play. All play is productive.

Children are asked what word they want to have for their own. This is easier done with naive slum kids, Indian kids, or other kids who haven't already been seduced by the reward/punishment structure of common instruction to give answers pleasing to the teacher. A *Teacher* will have to work to get natural replies from such kids.

As each child responds, the teacher quickly sketches out the word on a large card and gives it to the child, vigorously repeating the word. As she draws the letters she repeats—"Die." "Doggy-duh."

"Itchy-ih." "E-eek-a little scream." "Ghost." "Girly-Guh." "House-huh." "O-I'm surprised." "Hissy hissy S." "Toe-tuh."

She starts with all lower case. These associations, of course, are not sacrosanct. Any vivid association natural to the child is useful (but remember "pistol" was wrong for slum kids).

The teacher goes quite quickly until each child has his own card. The cards are collected sometime later in the day, and the next activity begins right after a quiet time, with the words accessible but no directions given about them.

On subsequent days the children get their own words out of the common stack of cards (after a vocabulary is built up, the older words can be kept and only four or five new ones put into the stack). The children will trade, but no attempt to cause this should be made. As each child comes up on the subsequent days, the teacher asks him to show his own card to her. If he doesn't immediately read them, she does. If he reads them, she says "That's right," if it is, or says the right word if it isn't.

Whenever the children ask for statements or sentences, the teacher goes right on and makes them on the card. If they don't ask (which would be an awfully repressed bunch of kids) she initiates by asking "Would you like to have more words at once?" but doesn't force coherent statements at first. Such kids are really crippled and should not be pushed.

After about six weeks the teacher can introduce MY BOOK made for each child out of poster board for covers with large sheets of newsprint inside. The child is asked if he would like to put his own words into his book. After writing a few, the teacher offers to write any little tale he would like to tell her. If the child doesn't even want to try to write at all, then she just goes ahead and asks "Well, what would you like me to write in your book for you?" Slowly, the amount of writing is increased at the pace of the individual child. This phase can come later for younger children and can be presented much more slowly. If the instruction is lively and successful, it ought to go quickly even with very young children.

If the teacher of older non-readers has a style which enables her to regress in this kind of instruction, it will work quite well even for very large boys.

MODERN READING is a style of instruction evolved by Hulda Regehr Clark and is enormously successful for both initial instruction and remedial work.

MODERN READING is based on the insights of developmental psychology. You don't have to teach an infant to see, although it is well known that infant vision is rudimentary. When chimpanzee infants were raised in total darkness, or in diffuse, undifferentiated lighting, they lost the ability to see, and in many cases the ability to relearn to see when shifted to a normal environment. Seeing teaches seeing. Seeing is learned by seeing.

Frederick the Great wanted to find out if infants raised without hearing a vulgar tongue would in fact grow up speaking Hebrew. Of course, he reared a couple of "normal" idiots.

If you watched a little embryo salamander you'd see the nerves grow out from the brain and spinal cord, literally boring their way through flesh, reaching the hands, feet, gut, skin, right to the most minute cell—right where it *ought* to be. We intuit that there is some sort of gene blueprint that lays all this out. The confounding thing is that if you transplant the tiny embryo hand—just cut it off and paste it back on to the back or side or belly—the nerve doesn't grow up to the stump and stop. Nor do nerves from the back or side or belly just grow up into the transplanted hand. The *proper* nerve changes its course of steerage and arrives at the hand wherever you might have put it. This hardly sounds like genetic unfolding.

Teeth seem to grow because of pressure from biting. Bodies seem to respond by growth in response to demands on them. Brains are larger, glial cells more complex and better insulated when environments are more complex.

Learning is a variety of growth. Body processes change, brain structures alter in response to the complexity and structures around the individual. Learning is not a product of intelligence, but rather intelligence comes about because of learning.

Think of teaching a ten month old to get downstairs safely. Explain?!! Just think, we don't yet have an educator that stupid. Well, how about an example? Just do it in front of him, running up and down just as he must? How about dramatization and excess? Visual aids? Programming? How about taking him up and down yourself? "First this leg, then this leg, ups and downsies?"

About a year, what? And, of course, at about the same time maturation has arrived so he might do it by any method of teaching or even with none. These examples are fairly close models of common teaching practices. We could have readiness techniques such as running in one spot, jumping from spot to spot in a floor game, or pedaling a bike. The major factors would be maturation and socialization just as it is for reading now, regardless of common technique—phonic or sight.

Now try this. During the ordinary course of a day upstairs you are ready to come down with your crawler, say to him:

"OUT?" or

"CAPTAIN KANGAROO?" or

"DADDY?" or

"CARS?"

or whatever fits your routine best, followed by "let's go see." Grasp his well-padded bottom firmly in your right hand, as your left balances his chest. Set him down on his tummy beside you on the steps, both facing the top of the stairs. Remember, you're in a hurry! Hold fast to his diaper or waistline and pull him down. If he's a fatty suspend him slightly. Step at a time, Swiftly, Bump, Bump, Bump! DON'T SAY A WORD! On to the bottom and off to see daddy or TV or what.

The chances are that he'll come right back to the stairs as soon as daddy or TV is over. So you pick up a magazine and sit down. When he's ready to come down or when your nerves can't take it, dash up there with a smile and grabbing his wiggly rear as before, say

"Downey, downey, downey, down" and pull him down as before. Do it swiftly. Don't worry about where his feet and hands go. They'll be finding themselves soon enough. Of course, you're stuck for the whole afternoon. And maybe the next day and next. But it won't take him more than five days to make it by himself.

Of course he's not ready for Mt. Everest, and you don't take him with you to the basement, or on the outside steps. Success is success enough for a while—say a month or two or even longer. And, of course, you don't haul in the neighbors to see! His joy is as much his own personal property as eyes and ears; sharing laughter and practice with brothers and sisters and daddy is enough. Learning is its own reward and showing off to relatives and neighbors is the beginning of the end of the real scholar.

By going downstairs, the infant learns going downstairs. By jumping and yelling he learns to verbalize. By jumping, yelling and seeing he learns to read. By reading he learns to understand what he reads.

These are the basic intuitions behind MODERN READING.

Many kids taught to read by the MODERN READING materials reach college level skill by age 10-11. We have not yet found a failure—*not one*. It does not require individual instruction, in fact it is not recommended to parents with a single child or for tutorial work. It works best with four to eight in lively groups outside the classroom.

This approach has no readiness criteria and no intelligence criteria (other than the enormously gross one that the child must be responsive—not necessarily verbally responsive). It works quite well from ages two on. The average six year old teaches himself in about three weeks (to the point of handling the simplest Easy Readers). Five year olds average three months of self-instruction.

The materials, which teachers can produce themselves, are a box of little books, the first of which have one or two big letters. The books are of various sizes and colors and while the letters are hand drawn the type is carefully reproduced with attention paid to distinguishing details on letters like "p," "b," "d," "n," "u" and so on. The books are given with recorded routines, one for each book. The procedure takes advantage of children's love to race and moves very quickly.

Each letter is presented as an identity with an association. "See the owl's eyes, oooo, say oo." "itchy, itchy, ih, say ih." The teacher ideally is only recording what happens, and the children move on to the next books as they master the first. No auxiliary subjects for language skills are used. Building, playing, music, art, math, games and lots of free flowing mingled conversation fill the class (no "hands up" or turn-talking).

The impressive thing is that children immediately are playing with the associations—if the teacher is well disciplined enough to follow instructions not to interfere. Children will spontaneously begin to print, and will ask everyone how to spell and then write the words. If the teacher hasn't made a chore of it, the kids write voluminously. Shy and withdrawn kids become much more outgoing, expressive and confident.

PRINCIPLES OF MODERN READING

1) Excitement, variety and vividness of presentation.

2) Presentation of bit by bit of data, one thing at a time, associated with data already known.

3) Learning its own reward—particularly testing and racing. Clark does give a little balloon or marble or other tiny toy at the end of each three minute session, but never after the races (tests).

4) Brevity of presentation (three minute classes).

5) Fast, fast, fast.

6) Withdrawal of teacher. Teacher's response not contingent on performance. Learning goes on apace regardless of *performance*. Remember, performing is what actors, musicians and seals do.

7) Matter of fact, easy (not evaluative—critical or gushy-sweet, but supportive) emotional climate.

ORGANIC/READING REMEDIATION grows naturally out of ORGANIC READING and MODERN READING. If the child is not a native English speaker teach him in natal language. Use comic books or anything else the pupil will respond to. Start with simple, well written fun comics—Casper, Wendy the Witch, Tom & Jerry, Woody Woodpecker, Hot Stuff. But quickly move on to the full range of comics including things you may think are garbage. We want these kids to read. If they read they will expand their reading. You might be amazed at the vocabulary counts in Marvel or other comics.

Write what the student has to say directly on an overhead projector. Make his captions for slides. Get a number of pans of hectograph reproducer and write up his story, immediately reproducing it for him and the class. Get a spirit duplicator. Make a day by day newspaper with very brief vivid stories. Do not censor any material. If you can't stand certain words think first of teaching other children. If you think you will want to stick it out then very matter of factly tell your children that these words frighten you and would they please lay off. Don't give them power over you by moralizing, or reacting blindly and irrationally. You are the professional. Would you like it if your doctor retched when he looked down your strep laden throat?

The important principle is to involve the children as directly, immediately and organically as possible, in an informal relaxed and purposive environment. Drill, readiness routines and textbooks are demonstrably destructive. Let the kids teach each other.

Regressing kids back to ORGANIC READING or MODERN READING tactics as if they had never had any reading exposure works quite well. We notice that the biggest problem with it is teachers' reluctance to work in such a childish way with big lugs. If the student's self respect is protected by telling him that this stuff is to help him teach younger kids the teacher may relax enough to use it.

I cannot too strongly emphasize that auxiliary language skills routines are a waste of time. Involvement with as many kids, workers, volunteers—people—as possible in free flowing conversations is all that's needed. With activity. Children love races, competition (competition with self, and with inanimate things), gadgets, activity, food, freedom from regulation, jokes and riddles, daredeviltry, amazing sights, rides, adventures, and ego inflation by success (NOT by compliment and praise). Kids hate evaluations, both praise and criticism, hate being made self-conscious, hate loss of dignity and control, immobility, regulations, being bored, most teachers, classes, schools and school work. One of the finest ways to achieve rapport with kids is to say "Well, I'm here to have a class with you in how to burn down the school." Never fails.

WRITE AND WRITE AND WRITE. One of the most effective means we have of working with adolescent failures is to make a daily 600 word essay the price of town privileges. The essays are cumulative (that is if you want to go to town on Friday you had to hand in five essays) but are forgiven at major holidays and ignored in the summer. The essays are not evaluated (so far as the student knows), corrected for spelling, content or grammar. The kids are encouraged to write anything at all so long as it is in the form of contiguous statements (we first got some lists of 600 "a"). The teacher tells them, "If you don't know what to write, write that. Write, I don't know what to write and I think this is a dumb thing to have to do and you are dumb for making me do it and I hate you." "Write anything at all."

In the last several years we have allowed kids to turn in 10 haiku (seventeen syllable poems) instead of the essay. Many delightful and rebellious books of examples are available which are greatly enjoyed by most teens. Again, no effort is made to grade or correct the haiku, although the pupils know that they are completely read.

For two years we have allowed kids to turn in 15 minutes of tape recorded talk instead of essays or haiku. What we are looking for is the constant production of work. Spelling, structural sophistication, grammar, and content all improve toward the norm of common usage as the student begins to produce, without any particular attention to these subjects by the teacher at all. Our students *must* achieve at the 85th percentile on the Iowa Tests of Educational Development for graduation. Their grammar scores invariably improve enormously. These are not merely subjective enthusiasms.

Daily production of cartoons, songs, artifacts, models or anything not made from a step-by-step plan would eventuate in improved writing skill. So long as the writing requirement is the simple price for a moderately important privilege, production will move in that direction. Of course, writing several disciplined essays and an extensive senior paper are among the prices for graduation at our schools. Kids have no difficulty adjusting to the idea of the essay as an organic requirement when it is presented as one of the sorry realities of life— "but that's it, Buster." We simply tell our kids, "If you can't do these simple things, then you obviously can't cope with the really important problems of the street." It seems important to us, however, that the choice *not* to write or produce be available for a very long time.

As a word of caution let me point out that ten percent of the children sent to us, both for residential schooling and in work directly in the slums or on reservations do require a step-by-step hand-holding primary routine. The advantage of giving them time to demonstrate that they need this kind of close instruction is that they diagnose themselves by their inability to operate in a program they enjoy, even when they don't seem to be producing in it. These zombie kids are all adolescents. We do not experience this kind of failure with kids under 12 or so—including kids seriously disordered, brain damaged, non-verbal and otherwise extremely far from success.

MATERIALS THAT TEACH

THE THIRD R is for some unknown reason the victim of a vast culture-wide neurosis. Nothing is easier than math. It is certainly intuited easily by babies. Yet, nearly every adult in our culture prides himself (and particularly herself) on mathematical stupidity. Why?

Probably because math is even closer than reading to skills like walking, and talking. (Look at all the stutterers we used to have; slowly we
see no more of them as the first Watsonian fad recedes. No doubt
we'll be getting a new generation of stutterers to add to the dyslexics,
etc., products of imbecile hurry-hurry schemes to teach three year
olds to read through anxiety driving.) Instruction probably destroys
math skills more quickly than reading skills. It's a good thing that
reading isn't so vulnerable or we would be in even worse trouble.

Math can be learned almost entirely through non-verbal means.
Teachers who attempt to remediate math failure through any means
other than those in the tradition pioneered by Cuisenaire and Gat-
tegno ought literally to be expelled from the profession. Cuisenaire
rods, Master cubes, construction sets, blocks, Think-sticks, geometric forms, house building, pool games, and most ball games, for
that matter, teach calculations, relationships, and geometry with a
great deal more elegance, intuitive power and productive accuracy
than any possible verbal means. The process of making these nonverbal skills articulate is simple, fundamentally related to the reading
systems described before, almost impossible of failure except by
wonderfully wrongheaded, and incredibly energetic miseducation.

Modern Math is, of course, only very old fashioned math come
into fashion again. Most Modern Math texts are quite good mathe-
matically so far as they go, but they seem to all be written by men
who have never taught or lived with small children, and they still include some incredibly dumb things. Why should children, in this day
and age, be taught four or five different notations for doing the same
thing? Multiplication, long and short division, fractions and decimals
are all the same function. If we are going to have to be stuck with
these functions because of cultural taboos then why at least can't they
be taught as a whole? Is there any reason for fractions to be separated
from division in the primary presentation? Of course, I have my own
primer to sell—so I am both prejudiced and have ulterior motives.

In verbalizing numbers and concepts one vivid idea at a time,
using money, in particular, or any physical objects, will rapidly build

an effective math competence. There is no pedagogically sound reason for not using fingers.

I prefer to use the fingers as an abacus with the right hand serving as units (the thumb is 5, and with it up then counting 6, 7, 8, 9 is easy on the one hand) and the left hand as tens (the thumb is 50 and with it up 60, 70, 80, 90 are possible on the one hand). A 99 cents abacus is perfectly easy to construct with four pennies, a nickel, four dimes and a half dollar (two quarters). Abacus play is great fun and a ready instrument for remedial instruction if it is kept free of association with the kind of arithmetic the pupil has already learned and which he found impossible and frustratingly fear-making.

If the teacher keeps in mind that all computations and relationships can be reduced to the simple operation of one plus one or its reverse then she will be able to relax about teaching numbers and computations. If the kids can be engaged in things that need adding or subtracting only and become quite fluent at these simple tasks, then multiplication and division will come with greater maturity and also be quite fluent. Keeping score, games like pool, cards, roulette wheels or other somewhat disapproved games are an excellent way of reaching older children and readily build computation skills. We refuse to use them only when we don't see the point in helping kids develop independently useful skills.

Let me hasten to add that research with Cuisenaire instruction has shown that children accelerate fantastically in the first three grades, but are about even with children taught by common methods by the eighth grade. This is to be expected since, in fact, the child does control the learning and teaching methods, the early presentation, and systems tend to normalize over a period of time. It is also to be expected since the excitement and relevance of the intuitive instruction is not maintained in grades 3-8. The points are two: Why shouldn't kids enjoy learning math if the method is at least as good as the commonly detested methods? And for remediation there is no other way that really works.

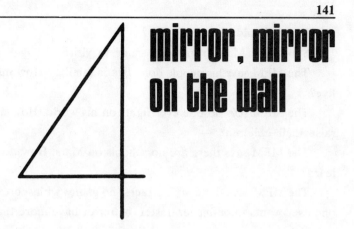

mirror, mirror on the wall

NEARLY ALL of the specific behavior interventions used in our programs can be divided into two categories: Skills building, and self awareness through confrontation. We find that self awareness, re-creating feedback loops through any methods that drive consciousness of what-in-fact-I-am-doing, enlarges control and causes the behavior of the individual to integrate and come under control.

I
MORE TALK

STRUCTURAL ANALYSIS: THE MAN FROM MARS. Verbal analysis, particularly by another person, of past behavior does not seem very useful. Verbal analysis of ongoing behavior and of commonly repeated behavior, particularly focusing on the interaction of the individual with others, does seem to control and shape behavior. This is particularly true of older, and verbally more intelligent students; however, the technique is useful, both for character training and achievement.

Ask the children to write, talk into a tape or discuss:

How you would organize the best school in the world.

What should a class be like?

Suppose a Man From Mars came to visit:

The MFM says his people don't live in families. How might they live?

The MFM says no one ever fights on his world. How must they raise their children?

The MFM says there are no schools on Mars. How do children learn?

The MFM says there are no races, no games with scores, and no one ever wants to be bigger, faster, better or have more than someone else. How must they raise their children? Why isn't it like that here? Do animals have races? Would you like that kind of way of being?

Talk about the kinds of ways there are of giving when people are together and don't have presents.

How many ways are there for people to say "Look at Me, Look at Me" when they are with others—without really saying it?

What happens so that people know who is the boss, or the leader? How do a group of children know, when they are all the same sex, age, size and grade?

What are ways for people to be angry but not shout and wave fists?

The MFM says he doesn't understand "Pretty." What is "Pretty?"

The MFM says he doesn't understand "Hate." What is "Hate?"

The MFM says he doesn't understand "Good." What is "Good?"

The MFM says he doesn't understand "Fail." What is "Fail?"

In all such exercises the teacher should not be directive, but may ask more and more questions. She should, after the students are comfortable with the game, bring the examples closer and closer to home and to the individuals.

How would you change what happened when you were in a group and it was angry? Could you show the MFM what "hate" means by describing how it is different from "love?" Who do you "hate?" Can people hate things? How is hate good—what is it good for?

The teacher should not "grade," approve or disapprove, but merely support production by indicating that she hears and understands, questioning for clarity or further penetration of the idea, and rephrasing both for understanding and for its own sake.

VERBAL TRACKING: CRISIS TEACHING. We are not convinced that crisis teaching is the ideal model for coping with crisis in the classroom. The disruptive child, the angry child, the conflicting child, the child acting out some craziness seems to us better dealt with in a milieu in which his unwanted behavior is controlled by simply being told "Look Buster, we are here to work and enjoy. If you don't want that, just go to the Freedom Room (or the Rec Room, or outside, or . . .)." It seems to us that the entire group is better served by dealing with emotional excess through a matter of fact rejection of it, control of it by ignoring it, control of it by giving it a simple reward without comment, or by having the group focus on it and decide what should be done. Many times, I simply tell the group "Look at John. Now everyone tell him, 'I see you John.'" Verbally exposing the tactic in a matter of fact, mildly ironic way, often seems to work. "Well, John, you want to play the disturbed game, it appears. Do you want us to give you some attention? Or is it affection you need now? What is it you want?"

Of course the teacher has to use some sense, but we have never seen a child harmed by asking the group to stop and talk about what is going on and how to cope with it.

On the other hand, there are many teaching situations in which this kind of rich structure is impossible. For reasons of administrative control, demands for orderly progression through set tasks, and other reasons unrelated to children's needs, even special classes are often prevented from doing what is merely sensible in the situation. Unfortunately, many administrators and teachers are committed to the "Well, you must *do* something" hysteria even when the literature is quite clear that there is nothing useful known that should be done. Something that *is* useful is the procedure of immediately removing the child who has transgressed, get him away from the group in a friendly, firm matter-of-fact way—unless he is really being a brat, in which case honest anger is almost always more relevant and effective than a tightly controlled and heated "cool." With the child removed, the teacher seeks to maintain eyeball contact, holding the child gently until he is calm, then forces the child to track the entire event with utmost detail, clarity, personalization and concreteness. "Tell me just what happened, John." "Well, nothing." "John, something is always happening, what did you just do?" The teacher pushes and pushes, characteristically against a fog of bad memory, inattention, and incredibly abstract and generalized misdirection. The teacher should not be satisfied until she gets a good FAIR WITNESS description of the event. It does not seem necessary to dwell on the emotional history of the event so long as the specific actions are described.

The ideal model for this technique is for a specialist teacher or aide to serve a number of teachers, working as a tutor or remedial instructor during times of no crisis. This person frequently engages kids when they are happy, productive and purposively social, maintaining a naturally relaxed and cheerful interaction. The limitation of this model often is met when it reinforces the tactic of the disturbing child to demand attention effectively through his outbursts. When kids are well aware that they are going to get adult attention primarily for success, happiness, productivity, relaxation, and joyfulness, their teacher has accomplished a critically important task. The teacher whose threshold is too low will have as unproductive a classroom as the teacher who totally ignores everything. The teacher can emotionally "ignore" behavior even as she removes a child from the room—without a word to him and without even looking at him. The teacher can "ignore" a behavior even as she flicks a look, or mutters, "If you want me to be a cop I will."

THE USES OF MORAL HONESTY. We have found that very vigorous exposure of a disturbing, thieving, disruptive brat in a very judgmental way is quite effective. A teacher should not make this her only tactic, but a simple transaction with a brat on the basis of "You

are a miserable little snot" turns out to be an excellent recommenda-
tion. We remain deeply impressed with the usefulness of moral
honesty. If a teacher is outraged at a behavior she can say so. Of
course her outrages ought not to be so constant that she is always
blasting at kids—if she can't take mere noise, disorder, sloppiness,
etc., she shouldn't be working with *any* kids. When a teacher is satisfied that she has been fair, has been doing her best to help a child,
and the child just simply persists in behavior that shows he is not
going to treat the teacher with good faith, then nothing will work if
the teacher does not communicate her disgust, outrage, and disciplined anger to the student. This is, of course, not productive for
the child who is extremely disordered, hallucinating, clothes tearing,
defecating, etc. Otherwise, our experience is that it may be damned
essential for the adult and certainly isn't going to harm the child.

Teen delinquents are very contemptuous of the "cool" of the
usual social worker and therapist, and receive that detachment as a
particularly destructive kind of violence to their integrity. While the
teacher needs to avoid being completely vulnerable to the child, a
solid display of honest anger, moral outrage, is often the only thing
that cuts through.

With the usual range of kids seen in day programs, and the larg-
est majority of disturbing kids in mental hospital programs and residential treatment centers, an essential approach is one that bluntly
names a moral spade a moral spade, and insists that the child does
have moral responsibility and control. In general, difficult children
respond positively to a mild ironic ejaculated criticism—"you bum,
you ugly, you nut, you schizo." An effective worker with such brats
has an easy relationship of tease with them. The tease can also be
moved into a very simple and matter-of-fact comment that a thief is
after all a thief.

One of the first discussions children hear after being sent to us is
summed up as: "Look, we don't believe in emotional disturbance. If
you want to see someone emotionally disturbed, just push my buttons. The fact that your mother was mean to you has nothing to do

with the fact that you are stealing from me, or refusing to work, or just being a bum." Such discussions, of course, have to be simple, have to be given by someone the kids can see as related to them in some way more relevant than the office consultation, and have to be completely free of treacley sweet ooze, and pious hypocrisy. Nothing is less useful than a "Sweet Jesus" talk. Such kids have nothing but contempt for the usual symbols of authority. A new, brusque, effective authority can penetrate their world and has to be made. In our experience such confrontations are best made by a strong male, whose ability to scorch in language is not limited to tea party vocabulary.

It is also important that these kids be forced to see that their own arbitrary behavior is just what they are rejecting. Visitors are often impressed by the sudden effectiveness of an immediate confrontation a newly arrived psychopathic boy might have with something like, "You are nothing but a lousy, stinking, foul, bribe-taking cop. You're like every frightened punk spoiled cop that ever stood on a corner banging heads with his club. You're a bum. Nothing is worse than a filthy crooked cop." There is no need in such a created crisis to complete the image of cops. The need is to penetrate his value world and make him see he might be exactly the thing he thinks he hates.

In general our experience insists that such moral confrontations are best made in the ongoing process of the day, during meetings in which all the kids are assembled to solve their problems, at the moment of a theft or denial, or when the brat is first seen after thoroughly verifying a betrayal. Confrontations can usefully be made during a group engagement called therapy, but we do not utilize these games at our centers. It is not essential that the teacher use the language style of the kids; however, it does seem essential to have a teacher or other worker available in the program to whom this style is comfortable and natural. Very little is worse than a teacher playing at being "authentic."

It ought to be obvious that the more vigorous applications of these transactions are not useful for quiet, shy, repressed, frightened,

depressed, or inward children. Most kids in public schools are repressed and frightened. Mild comments on the way in which the child
uses his depression, unhappiness, fear, and withdrawal are quite relevant and useful. It is particularly useful to respond to suicide threats
with just such excoriating moral outrage, verbal descriptions of the
unpleasantness and ugliness of death and corruption, and the firm
promise of the worker to see that no nobility exists in such a death,
and that the parents will be protected as completely as possible. "I'll
tell them how much better off they are, and you are. Isn't it much
better that he is safely dead than spending a lifetime miserably in pri-
son or the hospital . . . ?" Suicide threats are the lowest form of
moral blackmail; they can only work against people who love you
and the threatener knows this. Such situations are just about the only
ones in which we are aggressive and morally abusive to tender,
depressive and "well-behaved" distressed kids.

II
POOR LITTLE ME
I'M JUST A VICTIM OF MY SYMPTOMS

In many ways, we observe the compulsive person apparently de-
nying his identity as a free entity. He is saying, "I am just a bunch of
symptoms. I have no control, therefore no responsibility." The techniques that follow were evolved out of this insight and are means of
confrontation that demonstrate control over symptoms and enable
them to be eradicated.

COUNTING. Nearly any discrete behavior that can be separated
from other behaviors and counted can be reduced and eventually
eradicated by the process of counting it. We have obtained many records of the abolition of cigarette smoking through nothing more
complicated than obtaining the smoker's cooperation in recording
(usually on a wristwatch type golf scorekeeper) the number of cigarettes smoked with daily totals. The disadvantages of this technique
are that it requires active cooperation and persistence, it doesn't
work very fast, and it is not applicable to complex behaviors that are

hard to identify for discrete counts. Still, for the well motivated person trapped into a mildly undesirable behavior by habit or trauma it is an inoffensive and useful tactic. In a group it is a helpful way of enlarging everyone's awareness of all transactions, and of obtaining records so that the teacher or other behavior technician can design more powerful interventions.

If counting the behavior does not work too well, don't give up. A slight change in the procedure may still have the desired effect. Keeping a diary which lists the counted numbers of undesired events across many days, results in a *reducing* rate of the events in question. While *reduction* in rate may mean "success" to some people, others may not feel that reduced rates mean success. With such people, getting them to count time-off the symptom (e.g., counting 15 minute periods in which the person does *not* smoke) and recording these numbers daily, may work where symptom counting may not.

TINKLE BELL AND OTHER ALARMS. Much useless and destructive behavior is merely bad habit. Almost all habits can be broken up by vividly focusing attention on them. If you doubt this merely direct your attention strongly to exactly what you are doing the next time you go downstairs. It will be a good idea to keep a firm grip on the banister. Simple alarms that automatically or through the surveillance of a technician draw attention to a habit will have the effect of breaking up the habit. This is particularly true if another habit is substituted.

The most well-known application of this technique is the bell and pad alarm method of controlling bed wetting. Once a physician has determined that the wetting does not have an organic cause, a bell is established near the bed with its circuit attached to a pair of cloth-covered foil or screen sheets. When the first drop of urine strikes the sheet the bell goes off, awakening the child. Best results are guaranteed when the parent or technician sleeps near the child and wakes with the bell, making sure the child awakes, and seeing that he then goes to the toilet. If an older person is being trained and does not have assistance it is imperative that he is instructed to make an effort thoroughly to arouse and to go to the toilet when the alarm rings. Sometimes a physician must supervise a drug regimen so that awakening is facilitated. There have been thousands of reports on this procedure. There is no evidence of symptom substitution. The number of relapses is small and they are usually very easily re-trained.

A teacher can provide herself with bell, buzzer, ding dong, tone or other distinctive sounds, together with distinctive lights and a switch that readily controls the entire room's lighting. These signals can assist in eradicating or establishing specific behaviors merely by strongly associating the alarms with the behavior and a discussion of what goals are wanted. As in all of these techniques, the child can be fully informed about what the goal is and his understanding of the process can accelerate his improvement. No effective course with children depends on mystery. Mysteries are for fun.

NEGATIVE INSTRUCTION. Mark Twain wrote the definitive description of this technique. Forbidding an object makes it desirable. Commanding a behavior often makes it undesirable. We find that bed wetting can be more quickly eradicated by having the mother or house parent make up the bed carefully and then in full seriousness insist that the child wet the bed deliberately. No comments other than those directing the bed wetting are useful and no sarcasm should creep into the instruction. The mother simply repeats "I am really serious you must pee on the bed. Right now!" It is much more effective if the parent uses the term for urination that is the private, peer term.

The same approach works quite well for fatties. The technician simply instructs the child "I want you to gain five pounds this week. Before you come back for your next talk, you must gain five pounds for me. It's important that you do this."

Insomnia will also respond to negative instruction, particularly if some mildly unpleasant task is suggested as the means of assisting the person to remain awake. Simply instruct them that you want them to try to stay awake as long as possible each night. Of course, you will seldom hear complaints of sleeplessness from kids under college age—they are usually quite happy with sleeplessness.

The classical technique for eradication of stuttering and stammering is simply to encourage the child to do so. No sarcasm must be present but serious and insistent direction to try to stutter as much as you can. It constantly amazes me to learn that Wendell Johnson's work is not routinely taught to all workers with people, but there you are. We seem to have a dedication to complicating simple processes and to researching where none is needed.

Nearly all forms of undesired and undesirable behavior will respond rapidly to negative instruction. A related technique quite as powerful is to reward bad behavior. Without any discussion at all, simply give a bed wetter a quarter. If he asks "What's this for?" respond with a simple "You know." Thieves, swearers, bullies and others will rapidly respond to being rewarded for their bad actions. If the problem is a social one—thieves and bullies—it is of course essential to reward the victims as well. Often the bully's victims are just as culpable in any case; if you are going to be consistent, help them too. It is not wise to use this technique too regularly. There are times when I believe that the best thing the teacher can do is keep the kids completely off base. It may be that this technique works only because it just surprises the kid. It does work very well.

If you leave a playroom with the injunction, "Look, I'd like it if you didn't play with the ferris wheel," it is certain that far fewer children will play with the ferris wheel than if you leave the room with the injunction, "Look, I don't want you to play with the ferris wheel. If you do, I'm going to be awfully mad, I'm going to collect all the toys and I'm going to think you are babies." A strong threat enhances the value of an action or object. Teachers should know that symbolic threats, teasing threats (I'll paint you blue if you do that), and symbolic punishments are much more effective than strong real punishments.

One teacher of our acquaintance maintains good class discipline by symbolic punishments on the order of cutting out a black whip from construction paper and carrying out a mock whipping. He also has a firing squad with dart guns or water pistols. In effect he is saying to the child "Look, you and I know exactly what you are doing. You know it is forbidden. I know it. But I do like you so I'm going to remind you in this enjoyable way."

Our student/staff meetings frequently cause kids to wear funny signs: "I'm a Big Hero—I Smuggle Beer"; "I'm a Big Man—I Peek"; "I'm Sophisticated—I Smoke Grass"; "Dig Me—I Went To Jail." Heavy sarcasm, particularly from staff, is received as punishment most foul. Discussion and sermonizing are boring and not useful. Moral outrage must come as an outburst, or a cold, serious, and preferably vicious excoriation. Outrage ought to be reserved for problems more serious than stealing, beer smuggling, noise making, etc. More reasonable issues for moral outrage are sheer unrelieved contempt for you, drug using, violence and conflict mongering, contemptuous lying to peers, betrayal and sexual exploitations.

We deprecate the importance of negative behavior, particularly those actions seen by the kids as "big deals." This is essential. It assures that the peer culture doesn't maintain a delinquent and anti-social ethic that would be much stronger than any adult intervention. We find that regular student-staff meetings, given real authority, do penetrate the peer culture, especially when the verbally most agile staff can from time to time jeer at heroes, expose "corrupt cops," and bluntly condemn bums, thus effectively deprecating the importance of "adventures." The meeting, however, must accept real authority, and the teacher or administration *must be willing for it to make mistakes.* We create a conflict system in which the administration bluntly says, "You police the rules, including those the state and the administration makes. If you don't police the rules and deal with transgressors, then *we* will, and we will do it as efficiently as possible. We have no need to be liked, to be fair, or even right. If you are going to be in conflict with "cops" all your life, you had better learn now that cops can never have all the information, are usually scared silly because they don't know what creeps are going to do, and are very likely to

overact for very good reasons. That's just the way we intend to be."
Then, of course, the staff has to work, learning to see the meeting as a
class and not a place to defend their own ego or see that "justice" is
done. They must create a climate of non-punitiveness, be willing to
make ridiculous motions themselves, suggest symbolic and funny
punishments. They must keep the action purposeful and fun, the
tempo quick-time.

DIRECT FEEDBACK. Tape recording and immediately
replaying outbursts, the whining and importuning of little kids, self
hating statements, or other ineffective statements about self, is most
effective. Video taping created crises, role playing, simple
movements, making faces, psychokinetic routines, reactions to manipulations or spontaneous scenes, and immediately and repeatedly
playing them back, is very useful. Taking Polaroid shots of confrontations, postures, faces or other communicative poses and immediately giving them to the child is a productive technique. Movies
have the disadvantage of delay in time, but are less expensive than
T V systems and are quite useful despite the delay.

The child can be asked to look into a mirror and to describe
everything he sees. Then to evaluate and say which parts he likes and
which he doesn't. Then to make faces, but keep checking to see if his
eyes are in fact on the image.

MIMICRY AND ACTED FEEDBACK. A powerful in-
tervention is often one in which the teacher just stops everything and
does exactly what the child is doing. This is particularly effective for
the tantrums of problem children, particularly if the teacher can
really get into it, falling on the floor and doing the whole bit. It also
has the advantages of relieving the teacher's feelings. Acting back in
mimicry, even sarcastic mimicry, of hysteric or histrionic demands
and outburst can often be an effective means of getting control. It
exposes the kid's techniques, helps him witness its childishness and
funniness. Sometimes just falling on the floor and overacting hilarity
at a routine a child is putting on is the most effective thing to be done.
Humor, particularly if it is not biting and destructive, is a powerful

tool. However, the bosun's advice to the new ensign is very good for kids. "Men hate sarcasm. And they hate to be bulkheaded." Bulkheading, for your information, is to talk about someone in front of them as if they weren't there but were just the wall (or bulkhead). Mimicry at least shows that someone accepts him for real.

Despite the dangers of sarcasm (which is always less harmful from peers) a good way of dealing with a crisis is, after stopping it, to have other children re-enact the immediate drama. Having a contest among other children to see which team gets the action just right is not only fun for all, but instructive both to the participants and observers.

ELECTRONIC FEEDBACK. A technique available only to well funded enterprises, or those with a good electronic technician and lab available, is that of direct electronic feedback. Readers who mouth, sound-out, or subvocalize in reading can be diagnosed by having mesh electrodes placed over the carotid region of the throat and fed back through a very high gain amplifier to a speaker. Anyone with such bad habits will produce varying static as he reads. This process can be explained, a simple demonstration made of different levels of static by whispering, talking to yourself, reading and not reading. The student is then asked to read so that he produces as little static as possible. In about half an hour most cases are retrained with little relapse.

Muscle relaxation or other fine muscular control can be trained through the same tactic. Tics can be eliminated, as can other undesired movements.

It is possible for general relaxation and calmness to be trained by feeding back EEG signals through an oscilloscope so that the student can gain control through watching the actual wave pattern. Such training might be a more useful activity for psychologists on your staff than talking with kids or giving them tests. This equipment is available at less than $300.00

A CLINIC FOR CIGARETTE SMOKERS:
IDEAL MODEL FOR BEHAVIORAL CHANGE

Cigarette smoking is generally regarded as a foolish and dangerous habit. It is peculiarly resistant to all forms of education and particularly resistant to psychotherapy.

Cigarette smoking ought to be an admirable behavior for demonstrating the usefulness or irrelevance of any education tactic. The criterion for outcome are simple—no smoking after reeducation.

The following model has been successfully applied, using volunteers with two hours of training backed up by a simple manual on a range of subjects. It is now offered in a "money-back guarantee clinic" by Humanitas Systems.

All presentations of this clinic should be made by a person thoroughly convinced of their efficacy. The means by which the conviction is transmitted to the audience are immaterial. However, a "salesman" with rather aggressive, antagonistic, negative personality patterns will induce wider commitment to the change than a more pleasant person. No difference in numbers of groups accepting the project, or in volunteers for teaching has been shown in response to presentations by various "salesman." There is a clear tendency for those introduced by the convinced but somewhat negative personality to be more successful than those introduced by a more charming personality.

Once the clinic is adopted as a project it is important that the persons introducing the reeducation program to the students be convinced and enthusiastic. The student, introduced by a somewhat negative and brusque personality, will more thoroughly accept the program and the reeducation will take more quickly.

SESSION ONE: The student is given a brief orientation in the powerful tactics of behavior modification. Discuss animal behavior labs, cure of alcoholism, training astronauts. The importance of cigarette smoking should be deprecated. No attempt to build awareness of health hazards or other negative aspects of cigarette smoking should be made. The student pays a fee (about $12 per session) and is told that his money will be refunded if he is smoking six weeks after the end of the reeducation program. He will be given a free recycle with different techniques if he is smoking at the end of six months. The student can be required to make a deposit that will be forfeited if he does not complete the program. If a deposit is required the teacher should emphasize that this is to prevent the student from wasting time since it is too valuable, and too many people want to stop smoking to waste valuable teaching facilities.

If the student is married, the cooperation of the spouse should be enlisted. If the cooperation of business associates can be enlisted, do so. All associates and relatives of the student should encourage him to smoke as much as possible (not in an excessive or sarcastic way, but more than usual). No one should encourage him to stop smoking in any way. The spouse should be encouraged to light cigarettes, to have them readily at hand, and in every possible way to make cigarettes accessible and easy to smoke.

The student can be given a cigarette pack holder prepared so that when the top is removed a tiny buzzer or beep sounds.

Alternatively, a pack can be prepared so that a small shock, just below the pain threshold, is delivered on a randomized ½ sec. to 3 sec. or not at all after the holder top is removed. Neither of these preparations are essential. Cartons of cigarettes are prepared, using the regular brand, so that one cigarette per pack includes a fully disguised heavy smoke pellet from a novelty shop.

The student is given a wrist worn golf counter and instructed to count each cigarette smoked during the day and to make a record of it each night. The teacher should telephone once or twice each day, and each evening to remind the student to count and record the total each day.

SESSION TWO: One week later: The student will be instructed to continue the routine from Session One, and during this session will for one hour be asked to smoke at a normal pace but lighting and smoking two cigarettes each time. He is asked to smoke two cigarettes every time he has the urge to smoke during the week. He is instructed this week to count on the golf scorer each 15 minutes he does not smoke. The teacher phones reminders both to smoke two cigarettes each time and to count 15 minutes of no smoking.

SESSION THREE: One week later: Student is asked to smoke one cigarette after another, chain smoking, for 30 minutes. The teacher describes, out loud, every behavior observed. "Now you are reaching into your pack for a cigarette, you feel the cigarette in your fingers, you are reaching for a match, you have the match and are striking it, you can feel the heat from the match, you are putting the cigarette into your mouth, you can feel the tip between your lips, you are beginning to be annoyed at all my talk, you are inhaling the smoke, etc., etc." Every attempt must be made for the student to focus on every behavior and feeling during the class. Counting and smoking two cigarettes is continued during the week with the teacher phoning reminders as well as the routine from Session One.

SESSION FOUR: Electrodes are attached to the student's finger. As the student reaches for a cigarette, the stimulus is brought very slowly up and continues up through lighting, inhaling and exhaling. As soon as the exhalation is *completed,* the teacher counts silently one and two and three and four and tells the student to stub out the cigarette, or put it down, and immediately on releasing the cigarette the current is stopped. If the pain becomes too intense at any point and the student asks the teacher to stop, the teacher should tell the student to put out the cigarette or put it down and stop. Do not stop the current during exhalation or immediately as exhaling is finished—count to four after the breath is expelled or you will increase smoking subsequently. This session should go on for about 15 minutes. As it goes on, the teacher should ask the student to increase the expression of disgust toward the cigarette as he puts it down or out. The student should be asked to say "Gee, I don't really want a cigarette after all" or any other statement comfortable and natural for him to say, as he puts the cigarette down or out during the second half of the session (expression of disgust toward cigarettes continues). Counting and smoking two cigarettes is continued during the week, along with procedures from Session One, with the teacher phoning reminders.

SESSION FIVE: As the students sit comfortably at a table the teacher asks him to remember the last time he was hung over, violently nauseous and throwing up. The teacher builds a verbal image about the puking (it is important that everyday language comfortable for the student be used in this session), and particularly the nausea preceding it. The teacher talks of an association with cigarettes as the nausea image is building up ("remember how your throat felt, just remember that cigarettes make you feel like that, think how nauseated you felt and how horrible cigarettes made you feel, do you remember how your head felt, think about how sick you felt, cigarettes make you feel like that, etc., etc., etc.") It is important for the nausea feelings to be strongly built up. A number of students will actually become ill, so it is best to be prepared. During the second half of this 15-30 minute session introduce some relief by associating the putting down of a cigarette, the rejecting of a cigarette, etc., with the relief that came after being sick; but keep the nausea image building throughout the session. It is important to be specific and concrete; associate with an actual idea of a cigarette, not smoking in general. Continue other routines during the week.

By this time 90% should have stopped smoking. Those still resistant as reported in Session Six, should have as their Sixth Session a repeat of the class which was most effective as reported on their count records. If their biggest drop was during the first week, which is quite likely, then use the technique next most successful.

SESSIONS SIX THROUGH TEN: There should always be repetitions of the most successful techniques in Sessions Two through Five. Students who are still smoking should then have intensified (every other day) repetitions of Session Five (unless the record shows they increased after Five which will happen in a few cases), in which case, Session Four should be used (also unless increase followed during that week).

SESSIONS SEVENTEEN THROUGH TWENTY-FOUR: Intensify repetition of Session Five.

SESSION TWENTY-FIVE: Any student still smoking at this stage is unusual indeed. The teacher will have to decide which procedure has been most effective to date and intensify it (except that it will not be useful to have classes more than every other day). Disinhibition procedures will work very well for resistant students using stimuli for death, anger, dirt, exhibitionism, authority, accident, closeness and dependence.

Any one of the sessions can be used as the entire program and will work on 85% of smokers in sixteen sessions. The electrical devices are not necessary.

Relapses can be phased in at the point (in Sessions One-Five) they enjoyed the most success. The teacher simply replays the most successful session until the habit stops.

Seriously resistant individuals will very likely prove to have a very high pain threshold (measured by the electric stimulator) and a moderately high skin resistance as measured by a Galvanic Skin Response Meter. For these individuals direct punishment or aversive therapy may be useful.

During the first aversion session the student is told that he will receive a shock any time he reaches for a cigarette and that the shock will continue until he puts the cigarette down. The shock should be set just at the threshold of pain (strong pain is less effective for training than weak pain). The student should be instructed to reach for the cigarette as often as he can during the 20 minute session. If the student continues to hold the cigarette the shock should be continued and intensified slowly.

A cooperative, intelligent student can be given a small self shocker and instructed to press a small button that will deliver a short, sharp shock to his finger every time he thinks of a cigarette or starts to get one. This is a relatively quick technique for an intelligent, cooperative student.

A longer aversive session should take about an hour and the student should be shocked on a random schedule alternating among:

1) reaching for the cigarette;

2) five second delay after the student picks up the cigarette;

3) ten second delay;

4) no shock (if when not shocked the student lights up and starts to smoke then he should be shocked about five seconds after the third exhalation and the shock intensified until the cigarette is put out). This schedule should be randomized and at least one cigarette out of five should receive no shock at all and the student be allowed to finish.

III
DIRECT ELIMINATION OF FEARS

TERROR THERAPY. The Principle of Overload. Good results can be obtained in eradicating specific phobias or fears of students by use of the principle of overload or exhaustion. A terror of rats, snakes, spiders, heights, closed places or other phobias can be neutralized during several half hour sessions of tape recorded instructions. We focus attention on verbal constructs and thoughts of the most terrifying possible imagery associated with the object feared, interactions with it and emotions that might be experienced. A regimen that covers a broad range of fears given every other day has wide applicability. A simple questionnaire listing possible fears with a weight of one to six for the amount of each individual fear will give direct guidance for reeducation.

Such routines can be done in person but there seems little reason to do so. Group presentation through earphones has the advantage of enhancing the emotional privacy of the experience, and keeping an objective straightforward presentation unaffected by the technician's possible interaction with the student.

A brutal, direct confrontation can be built around a students ordinary rationalizations for self-hate and deprecation. Vivid imagery carried on for ten, fifteen or even thirty minutes will have much the same effect, making his rationalizations unacceptable and eliminating them from his characteristic style.

Some teachers in programs with extremely criminal students may find physical violence an effective alternative to some of the more passive, but emotionally more extreme techniques such as isolation, heavy sedation, discharge to adult maximum security prisons, etc. Physical punishment seems effective in two kinds of situations:

1. Where there are repeated petty crimes such as wife beating, bullying and petty thefts from friends or relatives, and particularly when the thefts are quite stupidly done; also when there is persistent involvement of weaker persons in crimes or self-destructive behavior (drugs, etc.). In this kind of behavior a very formal trial, exposure before peers (preferably involvement of close peers and most particularly peers who have been involved in misadventures with the culprit) formal condemnation, and sentencing are useful, perhaps critical. The punishment should be carried out in public, formally, and should be on the order of blows delivered to the back by a lath or rod held with elbow stiff and extended. The important dynamic is the repeated verbal statement of the offense, and the presence and involvement of peers. Every effort should be made to underline the contemptibility of the act.

2. Immediate, vivid outraged, overwhelming assault. In this kind of intervention it is essential that the teacher be: (a) Absolutely right, or in a situation where being wrong can be seen by the student as reasonable in view of his immediate and persistent history, the habitual patience, tolerance and good faith of the teacher, and the general loading of pressure on the teacher. But it is by all means better to be absolutely sure. (b) Honestly and thoroughly outraged, morally

revolted. This is hardly a technique to be turned on with utter objectivity, although it is possible that a consummate actor might pull it off. (c) The teacher must be of sufficient size, psychological strength or enraged enough psychologically to corner the student, completely flood his awareness, dominate his entire awareness. It is best physically to corner the student, and it is essential to force the student to keep constant eye contact with you. In general, the violence should be open handed and directed at the face. The teacher either has to be reacting to a situation so clear that there is no question about its content, or must be a completely fluent speaker able to batter, slash, tear, excoriate, villify, vituperate and in every other possible way tongue-lash the student, expressing as richly, earthily, pungently and directly as possible his evaluation, opinions and emotions about the culprit. It is best to engage the culprit in the act; however, immediacy can be recreated effectively by verbally recounting the crime and directing attention to it. It is essential that direct vivid contact be maintained throughout the crisis.

I realize that these paragraphs will prove horrifying to most teachers. Let me emphasize that I am talking about transgressors who have had at the very least a clear and thorough opportunity to enjoy the luxuries of freedom and the dignity of independence without policing. Such confrontations are certainly going to have no effect in a maximum security setting, or even in most general security settings or in public schools. It is essential that the confrontation be clearly the student's choice, in rejecting the trust, openness and good faith of an open campus and generally gentle supportive and fair milieu. It has become quite clear in our experience that a clustering of individuals will respond to no amount of good faith, charity, affection and good program. If these individuals are not to receive the ultimate violence of expulsion into a life inevitably leading to permanent incarceration, a moral and personal breakthrough must be made. *This is only about ten per cent of kids referred for residential care,* but for this ten per cent it is a critical intervention.

Our most recent statistical breakdown showed that 22 of 222

secondary age children had received direct physical violence. Only one staff member, myself, is permitted this tactic. Even in a small, special school, it is a delicate skill. For 20 the violent crisis was the watershed for their emotional growth and change toward adult transactions. With two I simply had the feeling that I didn't have their attention all during the "confrontation." Both were somewhat later withdrawn from the school, and both have subsequently improved, but we do not regard this improvement as a fundamental consequence of the violent confrontation. It could be. Of course, it helps to have a strong staff member take on the "heavy" role. The others play "aunt" or "uncle"—but never deny the intrinsic rightness of the judgement; they simply support the child as a child.

This is not a tactic to be used with young children—the individual ought to be near adult size and appearance unless he is extremely foul. Of course, "he" does not mean that females are excluded. With young children simply holding during crises seems quite effective. We have suffered a few incredibly psychopathic little boys—one 6 and one 9—who came close to our boundaries. However, these were the children of a psychologist and a psychiatrist, respectively, and fortunately this is not a large population.

In general kids at our centers understand that staff violence is almost always a consequence of:

1. Apprehension during drunkenness or drug use if the individual cannot quickly and alertly come into control, and if he persistently denies a blatant condition.

2. Clear evidence that the individual has conned another child into using drugs, particularly if the other child has never before used drugs. In this case he will receive violence even after the fact.

3. Violence to a smaller or weaker person.

4. Extremely contemptuous verbal behavior. (The rewards of this become less and less the longer a student is with us.)

5. Nearly any offense if the individual has been with us for about a year and has persisted in stupidly criminal behavior.

Since most of these students are psychopaths we are not concerned that our responses be perfectly consistent. We want to increase the ability of psychopaths to experience anxiety, and their need to control anxiety by purposive and social behavior. Moreover, negative reinforcement works most powerfully when randomly delivered for only about one-third of the behavioral lapses. Both these factors indicate that the more extreme the psychopathy the more deliberate the "inconsistency" of the controller.

Something less than ten per cent of students at our centers are, after a long time, designated by the students as "not subject to student control." These individuals, and one or two others who have relapsed to full blown drug usage in a culture of drug conniving, lying, cheating and betrayal, will be placed for varying lengths of time in a ward with full time night surveillance by the strongest possible staff member. Such individuals may receive violent reaction to the most trivial offense. The occasion of their placement in the ward is a time of extreme confrontation with verbal outrage and a detailed warning of consequences. Of course, removal from this setting must be attempted as soon as seems possible, and generally sooner than seems reasonable. Easy management is readily won with this procedure. Management is not enough though, and internal controls that operate in the absence of authority are essential.

Bear in mind that these individuals generally have only one alternative: life imprisonment. And they almost always have a history of behavior when in jail that leads them to solitary confinement or a less exquisite brutality than ours.

Violence, as a general thing, is useless or harmful. Sending kids off to the principal's office for paddling or verbal abuse is harmful. If violence is to be used it must be directed to the individual whose behavior is most likely to be reached by it, and must be used by an extremely gifted technician. It can usefully be used only in an environment of fairness, in which real, extensive and immediate trust has been given to the student—trust that results in risk to the staff, risk at least of discomfort and inconvenience if not more serious risk. It very likely can maximally be used only in an open, no walls, setting.

Still, I will not discharge staff for losing their temper and hitting a child. I will insist that the staff then take his lumps in the general meeting of staff and students. It is often less violent to smack a child than to compress and control the outrage felt. It would be absurd if staff could make much more important mistakes in verbal behavior, without even being noticed, and yet be discharged for isolated mistakes in motor behavior. Of course, someone whose style involved hitting kids persistently or hitting obviously inappropriate kids simply must go, immediately, and possibly violently. Certainly adults should not be free from consequences that direct outrage toward kids.

Makarenko tells a most liberating anecdote of his early months at the Gorki Colony. He had been given a small group of young male criminals, two or three staff, and a gutted, windowless mansion for a facility. After putting up with nearly every possible range of contempt and sloth from these boys, Makarenko admits that he flew into a rage and smashed one of the boys in the face when the boy refused to collect wood, but mostly because he called him by the familiar pronoun "thou." Makarenko was astonished that all these huge lunks then immediately and sheepishly went to work with a will. His own guilty reflections ("My God, what kind of philosophy of education have I discovered?") led him to believe that it was precisely because he had interacted with the boy finally not as an abstracted idealist, and not as a bureaucrat (who could, after all, have sent the boy off to jail as incorrigible) but with all the passion and honest feeling of a man. Makarenko also recounts a number of other "learning experiences" delightful for their honesty, and liberating in their underlining of the fact that no school, and certainly no school for difficult children, ever runs smoothly and in congruence with the ideals of its administration. Both Makarenko and I built as central to the philosophy of rehabilitation in our schools that we would never commit the violence of expelling a child because of crime or nastiness. Expulsion is a kind of ultimate violence.

APPROXIMATION AND DILUTION. The Technique of DISARMORING. *Dis*solving *A*nxious *R*esponses by *M*onitored *R*elaxation from *I*nhibit*ing* Stimuli (DISARMORING). This simple technique has proven enormously powerful in our programs, both for residential and day care. In this technique groups of slides are prepared in categories representing fears that we have found generally present and important in the character organization of difficult children. In addition tape recordings of sounds taken directly from a sound effects library, and tape recorded animals, descriptions of fearful situations, objects, memories, feelings, places and people are used. The slides are shown to the student after presentation of an awareness/relaxation tape, and the student has electrodes attached to his fingers or palm for a Galvanic Skin Reflex meter. If the slide elicits no negative response from the GSR the next slide is shown. If a negative response occurs then the technician waits until the meter recovers to a slightly higher value and then presents the next slide. Sounds or recordings are presented in the same fashion.

There are about eighty categories now being researched; however, in general we find the following to be adequate: Dirt, Anger, Aggression, Sex, Social Closeness (Separation), Death, Exhibitionism, Mothers, Authority, Distortion, Injury and Mutilation, Automobiles and Accidents, Success and Reward, Confinement, Water, Faces, Animals. Specific presentations can be built by selecting out of a large library those slides which cause reactions in the skin response.

Some study has been made monitoring these anxiety responses by pulse rate and blood pressure; however, the GSR seems sufficient.

The most satisfactory element of this procedure is that with moderate cost (about $2500) the entire process can be made automatic so that the student enters the room, places the electrodes on his hand, starts the recording, and the slides automatically go on, remain or change, depending on switching circuits responding to the GSR. Some complain that this is a horribly mechanical process, but this is a worse than silly prejudice. In fact, here we have maximum privacy of a therapeutic transaction. The student engages with the slides precisely at his own rate, dealing with exactly the material that he is ready to deal with, and only that material which is relevant to him. His total person controls the process completely as he interacts safely with the reality prepared by the teacher. His nervous system relearns appropriate responses to irrational fears and the process of auto-kinesis or self-cure is accelerated.

CONDITIONED ACCELERATION OF RESPONSES BY RELIEF FROM AVERSION (CARRA). Some students are too agita-ted at first to work well in the DISARMORING procedure. Many of the techniques previously discussed will work for such students, in-creasing calm, relaxation and control until cooperation with DIS-ARMORING can occur. A technique that works very well for in-creasing the responsiveness of withdrawn students, or objectifying and economizing the responses of hyperactive, over abstract or psychopathic students involves a simple procedure using electric stimulation. The procedure has been mentioned earlier and goes by the acronym CARRA.

A simple electric stimulator is demonstrated to the student. He is allowed to fool around with it, find his own sensation threshold and pain threshold. He is then told "I am going to turn this stimulator on and slowly turn the control so that the stimulation increases until you make the response I request. Then I will immediately turn it off. What I want you to do is to tell me something you might say to your mother when she wakes you up in the morning. Each time tell me something different."

The operator slowly turns up the current until the student com-pletes his response, counts "One" and releases the button or key. "Now another." The operator, having returned the control back to below the sensation threshold, then turns up the current again until the student completes his response. This procedure should not be carried on so long that the student experiences real difficulty thinking of a response. As soon as a really long pause occurs before the reac-tion, change categories.

Responses can be any simple situation, or even calling for de-

scriptions of things, names of things, or persons. They should preferably be conversational gambits with at least a small emotional
load. "What you might say if your father won't let you have the car."
"What you might say if your allowance is cut off." "What you might
say when you see a pretty girl." "What you might do or say if you saw
a car rushing at a kitten." "Think of some new nicknames for your
friends." "Describe your friends."

This procedure was developed to reeducate a woman with a full
verbal repertoire of five responses. That is, she would reply to any
question with "Doctor, it all started when I had TB " or "Doctor, I've
been thinking of committing suicide," or one of three other equally
inappropriate comments. Within three training sessions (given every
day for five minutes each), this woman was responding normally in
conversations, with a usual range of responses. After ten presentations she was administratively transferred to another ward, and she
promptly regressed. On retransfer she was quickly retrained and
eventually discharged without relapse after about six months of
CARRA and DISARMOR training along with training in feeling talk
and assertiveness.

INCREASED RELAXATION BY RELIEF FROM AVERSION
(IRRA). A related tactic is used with fairly agitated, tense or
dysphoric students with a great deal of patently visible but unexpressed fear. The same equipment is demonstrated to the student in
the same way. This time the student is instructed, "I want you to take
this current just as high as you can and when you want me to turn it
off say 'be calm'." The technician hearing the "be calm" counts "one"
then releases the key. Returning the control to a low value, he repeats
the process about 20 times. Each value is recorded so that a record is
made of the increase or decrease in tolerance for electric stimulation. The procedure should be given every other day. This procedure
is called anxiety-relief conditioning.

THE DINING ROOM AND BEDTIME. Our teachers are early
told that the dining room is the most important classroom we have.
The superior school requires staff to eat with the children in a setting

that is quiet, relaxed, controlled only by the purposive enjoyment of the staff who see that amenities and style are maintained. Some of the staff circulate, massaging shoulders, making small comments and otherwise associating their authority and adultness with a mealtime that is divorced from the common experience of difficult kids as it is possible to be. Our histories of children invariably include their own reports indicating how the experiences surrounding every primary material reinforcement in their lives are chaotic, unstable, tense, argumentative, punitive and otherwise unpleasant. Meals are occasions for criticism, reprimand, punishment and argument. Clothing is purchased fortuitiously on tense shopping trips accompanied by much turmoil and wrath. Allowances are generally haphazard, overgenerous on the whole, but fortuitously delivered and usually requiring nerving up before asking for the delivery of funds. Most rewards in these children's lives have been used to reinforce disorder, disobedience, conning, conniving, nervousness and overall a climate of anxiety, judgment and fear. The most effective tools teachers have are quiet involvements with kids at rewarding times, meals especially, with a stable, attractive and happy atmosphere.

Bedtime must be used, in the residential setting, as a time for emotional and supportive talk, contact, touching, and loving up play between adult and child—regardless of age. Nighttime should be conditioned into calmness, relaxation and peacefulness. Bedtime violations of curfew will rarely occur if staff is made available for active interaction at that time. Unfortunately, it is common practice to have the most qualified staff on duty between 9-5 and to abandon kids to admittedly inferior staff at night.

If the child is in day school or counseling, it may be that the parents can be induced, in the name of technique or treatment, to give physical loving up to their child at night. It seems strange that inducement might have to be required. Many parents, however, are quite repressed about physical contact even with their own children. Sleep will be greatly enhanced by vigorous tickling, massage, physical play, particularly physical play that attends to the long muscles of the back, shoulders, neck and legs. The direct dissolving of fears depends on reconstructing the fear-creating mechanisms in the child's daily life.

IV
REWARDS AND PUNISHMENTS:
THE CLUMSY BUT SOMETIMES USEFUL TACTIC
OF OPERANT CONDITIONING

Without going into the pros and cons of operant conditioning let me merely dogmatically say that it is in general an expensive, inappropriate technique difficult to bridge into other environments and general behavior. Just like the chicken that drops the token and starts scratching around, or the hog that drops the reward wafer and starts rooting around it, people are sometimes programmed in ways that don't fit the needs of the operant trainer.

Artificial or "token" economies were first reported by Homer Lane—who apparently was also the first psychoanalytic educator. However, Lane's token economy recreated an entire commonwealth inside his reform school with rent, clothing, food and all the material goods of life being earned in a social structure that also protected the nonperformer. Lane's system deeply involved the students in the entire operation of the school and involved the staff in real risks. The token economy therefore had a symbolic and real potency that patently stilted and partial economies cannot have. Still it is quite easy to gain management of behavior on a ward by setting up a reward system for work and appropriate behavior. It is helpful if a substantial percentage of all behavior is observed by careful workers and that a consistent but not invariable pattern of reward immediately follows the desired behavior. If the desired behavior is complex or formal (say, working in the laundry) then it should always be followed by a reward as contracted.

Behavior desired by a technician will be more strongly established if it is not rewarded every time but is intermittently rewarded on a randomized basis about two out of three times. Punishment will inhibit a behavior, if it immediately follows the behavior, but with much less force than reward for a positive behavior. The punishing effect will persist much longer if it too is offered on a randomized intermittent basis—at a lower ratio depending on how long the behavior will be punished. That is, if you have only 100 trials available to train out a behavior then the ratio of punishments should be about one in three trials; if you have 1000 trials it should be about one in ten after the first 100.

The operant principle works much more effectively when the engineering of a social situation abolishes the expected rewards built into the habitual behavior of authorities. Careful observation of a classroom or home will demonstrate how difficult behavior is easily caused by the attention of the adults and their characteristic responses to children. Most adults attend to children much more quickly when they are naughty, noisy, or nasty than when they are nice. It is a pleasant commentary on the essential goodness of children that they are not always naughty, noisy and nasty. If these characteristic behaviors ("Mama, can I have a cookie?" "No, dear." "Mama, I *want* a cookie!" "No, Honey." "AAAAAAAAAAAAA" "O.K. O.K. Here's a cookie.") can be abolished, the behavior of a child will immediately shift toward the norm. Ignoring bedtime tantrums for about nine days will abolish the tantrums but it will be done without ill effect on the child, unless some organic factor is involved.

ASSOCIATIVE REINFORCEMENT can be used to shape kinds of behavior which are not actually occurring. Homosexuality responds very well to a routine in which slides of homosexuals or attractive males are shown with increasing electric shock, then followed by either an attractive female or a neutral scene which stops the shock. The most powerful use of this approach allows the student to control the shift of the slide. The longer he looks at the male slide the higher the shock. When he switches to another slide the shock goes off. For some reason randomizing the alternation of women or neutral scenes seems more effective—that is, male slides may be followed by neutral or females, but never by another male.

Simple shock suddenly applied to the appearance of a male picture seems to work but less well. Various other obsessions will respond to treatment in this fashion.

In general, relief from pain or discomfort seems more powerful than simple reward or punishment.

Verbal associations also seem quite powerful. The technician instructs the student to imagine as vividly as possible the unwanted behavior. He then instructs the student to remember at the same time the most horrible nausea he ever had; sickness, weakness, pain, disability, and other unpleasant events are built into the imagery as the technician weaves the instructions around the image of the unwanted behavior. With behaviors like cigarette smoking the actual behavior can be associated with the verbal association. This technique is also available to stronger and verbally more intelligent persons for self-correction. In general, we use simple reward/punishment contingencies late in a treatment series, when other procedures have not worked. With apparently retarded individuals, rewards; with gross schizophrenics, punishment. Imbecile procedures like building twenty word vocabularies in autistic kids by reward/punishment contingencies are not used. The holding technique with lots of social play, mimicry, and feedback works much more quickly with nonverbal kids. Of course, if teachers have time while carrying out all the animally more healthy procedures, a reward/punishment structure for verbal production might be helpful with a very disordered mute but vocally intact child. It would be an autistic behavior itself to use it as the primary intervention.

Teachers would do well to remember that any desired behavior can be secured in a number of apparently mutually contradictory ways. For instance, if you, for some obscure reason of your own want to have a child keep still in his chair, and you have most of the children keeping still in chairs, you can train him by:

1) ignoring his leaving the chair;
2) having a peer talk him into staying in the chair;

3) having a new and respected authority talk him into the chair;

4) by overloading: verbally browbeat him into the chair;

5) rewarding his leaving the chair;

6) punishing his leaving the chair;

7) rewarding him for coming to the chair and then for each period of quiet in the chair;

8) putting various signs on him with various verbal comments;

9) having the class talk about why he won't sit in the chair and doing what they suggest;

10) standing on your head each time he gets out of the chair;

11) having hysterics when he gets out of the chair;

12) breaking down and crying when he gets out of the chair;

13) ring a bell when he gets out of the chair;

14) doing a different thing each time he gets out of the chair;

15) sound a ding dong when he approaches or sits in the chair;

16) doing different but very obviously unusual things on a schedule unrelated to his chair behavior;

17) tell him he must stay out of the chair.

Recording what in fact works with this lad will give you a partial insight into how he learns. It is certain that each of these kinds of behavior will shape the behavior of some child so long as the issue is clear, and there are at least ten other interventions clearly applicable: taking a film or picture of him; having the class draw a boy who can't sit in his chair; stopping him and having him describe exactly all the things he is doing and has been aware of for the past half minute and at that minute; asking everyone to get up each time he does; having one student get up each time he does; getting up yourself; you or someone following him around; having a "twitch in our chairs" game; stacking the chairs up and having everyone sit on the floor; turning the chairs upside down and having a march; having people pair up and sit on each other's laps', backs, feet, one on two; having everyone draw chairs on the board; having everyone cut chairs out of paper; going outside; recording an attention routine about sitting and playing it back; having someone demonstrate sitting to the class; having everyone try sitting naturally in front of the class and talking about how hard it is to do it; trying to think why the Man from Mars can't sit even though he has only two legs and walks like we do; having a jump and yell session.

The critical principles in all behavior change are those which underline enlarging *awareness,* enhancing *contact,* building *control* through feedback and mirroring, and enlarging *skills.*

The most therapeutic thing a teacher still has to do is to teach her kids how to read and write and be happy at it. All the rest is in service to the goal of building competence.

appendices

The Appendices on Remedial Reading and
Tips for Teen Age Volunteers were written by
Dr. Clark and are copyrighted by her. They
are reproduced here by permission.

Also included in the Appendix is a paper by
Sol D. Klotz, M.D., FACA, FAAA, FASI. It is
entitled "Putting Medicine Into The Medical
Model," and is reprinted here with permission.

appendix

GREEN VALLEY

AN ETHOLOGICAL APPROACH TO MAKING DISTURBING
CHILDREN MORE LIKELY TO BE PRODUCTIVE AND LESS
LIKELY TO SEEK PUNISHMENT, VIOLENCE, DISORDER, UN-
CONSCIOUSNESS AND DEATH

Some Insights from Rats

RATS ARE USUALLY NICER than people. This is especially true of
rats that live in the woods away from people. Catch some wild rats,
put them in a very large enclosure, and watch them. You will see very
effective beings. They spend most of their waking hours *living*—fully
active, working, having fun.

If the population isn't too large for the food supply, the rats run
about and climb, exploring. They play elaborate games all night long.
If you put running wheels in the enclosure the rats will climb in and
work away for hours. Try square running wheels which demand more
energy and precision. They will choose these square wheels over the
easier round ones. All this lovely work they do for nothing. And their
"useful" jobs get done very efficiently, as well—building nests, ga-
thering and storing food.

They are very good parents. The children are well behaved,
too.

Then you can force a very people kind of thing on them. Ordinarily when a researcher catches wild rats and puts them in a large enclosure he provides boxes and nesting material scattered about. But the "people thing" is a habit of "schooling"—like fish. So to make the rats school up, put the nesting boxes in a neat row, A-B-C-D, and fix it so that to get into nest B and C you have to enter thru A or D.

ONCE FORCED TO SCHOOL UP, the rats start acting very much like people. They greatly reduce their regular work/play routines. They fight a lot. They start ignoring their offspring, except every now and then to snarl or snap at them. In just three generations of ABCD nesting you note an enormous number of still births, miscarriages, cancer and other degenerative diseases, homosexuality and violence. Mothers will carelessly kick their babies out of the nest, and fail to notice them sprawled on the floor. Sometimes the babies get eaten. The nests are always bloody, active, noisy, squabbly. Pity the poor mouse that is let into the enclosure.

Put these rats in mazes; they are not as smart as rats raised in separated nests. They don't weigh as much. They prefer sucrose to thiamin rich foods. They don't live as long. Their cellular structure is not as complex. Their brains are smaller, with smaller glial cells.

Even if you remove ABCD rats to an enclosure with scattered nests they remain agitated, violent and less productive. Their grandchildren behave in much the same ways even though they and their parents were raised in independent nests.

Train ordinary rats to work for food independently. Put them together, and you will see them organize a hierarchy of workers. One rat will do much more work than another. ABCD rats *always* are loafers. When put in with other rats they frequently stage a mock battle, then just keel over and die. This also happens when different species of rats are put together, but happens more frequently with ABCD rats. Only a small percentage of rats are natural mouse killers in relaxed circumstances, but "schooled" ABCD rats always attack mice.

WE KNOW MANY OTHER WAYS to make rats and people

(not to mention kittens, monkeys, goats and other small creatures) irritable, agitated, violent, dumb, weak, susceptible to disease and lazy. Remove them from their mothers very early. Give them that sort of mother to start with. Force them to remain still or be quiet. Starve them. Flood them with lots of noise. Keep their surroundings simple and dull. Punish them frequently—and punish them especially for exploring and playing, for showing emotion, for acting spontaneously, or for touching or moving themselves.

A Matrix Theory of Disturbing Behavior

The factors molding destructive, disturbing behaviors can pretty well be identified. All forces of the matrix interact, but one may grip too tightly to be shaped by the other factors . . . until relieved. Any one cause may dominate. Let us arrange the causes we recognize in this order of probable strength:

1. genetic
2. constitutional
3. early kinetic interactions
4. early diet
5. complexity of surroundings
6. early training
7. cultural or situational givens
8. disease and dysfunction.

Now consider the following examples to see how each of these factors influences life and behavior:

1. (Genetic) A Tay Sachs child cannot survive. Hopi children are carried about for a long time and when they are first set down they run—they don't have to crawl before they walk.

2. (Constitutional) A Downs Syndrome child can't become a doctor. Premature babies almost always grow up with some liabilities. If mother was malnourished, or constantly under stress, or suffered repeated trauma, baby will grow up with some liabilities. There are "strong" and "weak" individuals.

3. (Early kinetic interactions) A chimp raised in the absence of light can't see, or can't see well; it won't even be able to learn to see. Horses raised in the usual way will freeze or panic in a fire; they will kill themselves when caught in a fence; they are generally pretty stupid, "neurotic" animals. But if their early training included holding, calming, petting and coaxing, they will be quite different. Babies raised without mothers or in isolation become pitiful.

4. (Early diet) A child who is very hungry during the first six months of life will not recover a wide variety of abilities. If his parents or grandparents were chronically hungry he will likely be deprived of skills.

5. (Complexity of surroundings) Animals raised in a cage have smaller brains, smaller glial cells, less competence of all kinds, than those raised in a complex or free environment.

6. (Early training) An ABCD rat will be damaged. Forest pygmy children do not have accidents. Arapesh adults can't express active rage. A Hutterite who becomes psychotic will not become paranoid or violent but will become depressive. An Okinawan won't suffer stress neurosis and can't force a child to do anything.

7. (Cultural or situational givens) A Zulu can't see straight lines. A desert Bedouin cannot see photographs as pictures. A Trobriander will die if he hears and believes certain common words. A Mundugumor born with his umbilical wrapped around his neck will be an artist, and no other Mundugumors will be as talented.

8. (Disease and dysfunction) Hypoglycemia, thyroid imbalance, electrolytic imbalance, iron deficiencies, other chemical or vitamin deficiencies, diabetes, allergies and other homeostatic disorders will often cause abberant, destructive, psychotic epileptic or other unusual behaviors—including death. They often do not. The same is true of growths and bacterial or viral diseases. Disorders and diseases often follow or accompany stress, trauma and emotional situations and styles. The matrix becomes extremely complex and dynamic at this point.

The Circus Versus the Zoological Garden

Perhaps it is completely unfair of us to do so but we contend that Green Valley's approach relates to ordinary school and hospital practice much as a modern, sophisticated zoological garden is related to a circus.

The circus master is interested in the performance of his animals for the audience. He is satisfied when the animals are healthy enough only to perform.

The school master is interested in the child's performance of certain set formal tasks. The admiration of the audience of parents and school boards satisfies him. He requires only that the performer be healthy and disciplined enough to arrive and perform.

The hospital administrator is concerned to deliver a tractable patient to a "doctor" for "treatment" an hour a day or week. The rest of the time is holding time.

The ETHOLOGIST, as administrator of an adequate zoological garden, is concerned to build and maintain an organic, "natural" environment. He wants the behavior of the animals to be as "natural" as possible. An ethologist knows that "natural" behavior is not a fixed entity: lions in Kenya did not hunt in groups 100 years ago but were solitary hunters; starlings didn't know how to open milk bottles on door stoops 100 years ago. Deer were almost extinct in the United States in 1900, but now seem to thrive on urban and highway disruption of the environment.

Primarily the ethologist wants to see how the animal solves all sorts of organic interaction problems. The critical factor is to avoid intervention while allowing a complex ecology to operate. He may well introduce a single element (a running wheel in an open field) to gain data; but his focus sharply defines the animal within its total economy.

At Green Valley we contend that we are
    biologists
    ethologists
    behaviorists

and that all of us are acting in some fashion as

> parents
>
> healers
>
> teachers.

Beyond that we are administrators, managers, bookkeepers, secretaries, pharmacists, drivers, carpenters, plumbers, electricians, boatmen, gardeners, cooks, maids, artists, craftsmen, writers, printers—all rather visibly involved in the subject's ecological, experiencing field.

We use the words *client, student, patient* or *child* quite interchangeably regardless of the individual's age or reason for being sent to us. Some primarily need remedial education; others are here because they deeply disturbed authorities.

Our ethological structure is built on existentially democratic ground. Nevertheless, the resident client-student-patient-child and his entire milieu depend on the institution. Our sunny ethological model is an ideal that can't just happen; it takes shape by staff manipulations. And it takes a great deal of effort to appear to be "doing nothing" in a zoo or hospital. But when called for, we find it important not to mince words about power and intervention with children.

Making the Human Garden Work

BIOLOGICAL inventory and regulation. It is stupid if not immoral to fail a hypoglycemic patient by not regulating his glucose supply. His brain had better be able to function before we offer him the choice of setting his own bedtime, regulating his own diet or learning how to read. A remedial diet often tells the whole story.

BOUNDARIES that are firm, clear, consistent and real. The child *knows* what and whom he can depend upon. It really doesn't seem to matter very much if the boundaries are actually fair, although it is nicer if they are. Sometimes, as the farmer said, a mule-headed client requires an attention-getting device like a two-by-four applied suddenly between the eyes. Tough, honest language often does it. After gaining his attention we give him a list of things to do, and we say, "Choose one." (At last analysis about ten per cent of our students were mules.)

TIME to relax, regularize, recuperate. The patient is almost certainly under chronic high arousal, has difficulty sleeping, is quick to startle, overreacts and has a badly regulated metabolism.

A good deal of doing nothing is often the first prescription.

GOOD SLEEP.

COMPETENT people who are warm, touching, friendly.

Everything else is aesthetics.

What To Do Until the Humans Come

A problem: warm, touching, friendly, competent people don't want to work with cold, aloof, frightened or angry, boring or incompetent children. The problem *may* be that there are no warm, etc. . . .

A wonderfully honest director of a good clinical center for disturbing children was recently at a convention workshop on "In-Service Training of Staff." He jeered at the panel: "What the hell are you talking about? I filled out 650 W-2 forms last year for only 120 jobs. Everyone I know of has the same problem."

Anyone who runs a place for children, including the nice, clean, orderly, posh boarding schools for nice, clean, orderly kids, has the problem. His staff is not perfect, and often not very long there.

For years Green Valley was able to reduce this problem by staffing only with disciplined members of a nonsectarian brotherhood (men and women). We can't do this 100% any more. It may be simply that when people can make $12,000 a year selling insurance or installing plumbing, they can't see making $600 a year working with children. Or it may be that the war against puberty is intensifying. In any case, no environment for children is staffed with enough adequate people.

This absolutely means that a clearcut philosophy and workable technology of administration, management, education and therapy must be followed. It all must come in steps at least as simple as those needed to run a garage and succeed in repairing cars.

We believe that we have brought this problem into scale by following a primarily biological approach within the framework of a democratically existential milieu. No particularly superhuman qualities are needed to work a technique by which a student's failure to perform yields a reduction of choice.

Arriving at Green Valley

A child who enters is told:

1. The only way out of here is to graduate. We never fail, expel, suspend or otherwise give up on people.

2. We don't believe in disturbed kids. If you want to see some disturbance, just punch one of my buttons. The fact that mommy was mean to you has nothing to do with the fact that you steal, or won't learn to read.

3. Your improvement, your learning, does not depend on you. We don't care if you are poorly motivated, lazy, dumb, uncooperative, mean, or whatever. *You will learn here.* We are teachers and we are going to teach you.

4. We start by assuming that you want to be an adult kind of person . . . that you hope to get out of here as soon as possible . . . that you want a diploma or certificate that means something—skills that lead to independence and income.

5. We will give you privacy. If you respect that privacy and other people's privacy you will keep a private room and the dignities of being adult.

6. You can prove that you are still in love with cops, probation officers, guidance counselors, therapists, social workers, psychologists, psychiatrists, etc., if you want to. Just keep on behaving like a baby or a bum. Then you will lose privacy, lose dignity, and may wind up finally in something that looks remarkably like a Marine Corps basic training camp.

7. If you prove that you are still in love with failure—that is, if you won't read or do anything constructive that might substitute for reading—then we will take you by the hand for the step by step climb up the ladder to adult competence. We have lots of space and things to work with—books, boats, cars, construction projects, you name it. You will graduate as a competent adult worker or become ready for the game of college.

8. The basic rule of the place is GOVERN YOURSELF OR BE GOVERNED BY US.

How It Works

Some patients are immediately recognized during the first comprehensive testing as biologically incapable of self-regulation (perhaps one in ten.) They live with young parents in as normal a house as possible, with every effort made to integrate them into the ongoing democratic life of the community. They are not expected to work beyond their own grooming and housekeeping. They do attend the community meetings although one or two are sometimes incapable of interaction.

Most students initially receive private rooms which they must maintain themselves. They can lose the room by filthy housekeeping or violating a rule of the community made by the general meeting. Students and staff members each have one vote at these meetings. The staff has been known to boycott the general meeting as a means of increasing tension and creating crises, a technique that raises the morale of the client population quite effectively.

Many children entering Green Valley immediately seem at home. The problems described in their histories do not appear. Right away they become purposively engaged and they soon graduate. It looks as if the essence of the structure in and of itself enables these children to regulate themselves without a lot of to-do. Old habits lose meaning and fade quickly.

Others are here for months and remain unproductive, dishonest, lazy, bored, agitated and destructive. They resist the milieu, and must be more thoroughly assessed. Frequently these children need biological regulation. Psychomotor or perceptual dysfunctions call for remedial work in fundamental learning skills. Still others are harboring lifelong chronic stress or traumatic conditioning which requires specific behavior modification routines. There are workable techniques to enhance neural homeostasis, to desensitize phobic material, to increase perception and to enable more precise and accurate assessment of the surrounding world. These routines are now organized to the point that they can readily be administered by aides and other personnel under psychiatric or psychological supervision. In many cases the routines can even be automated, and require only technical and maintenance personnel.

For a precise or detailed description of the Green Valley interpretation of behavior modification we suggest that you read: *Is There a Science of Behavior,* $2.50; *The Teacher as Behavior Engineer,* $.50; *A Field Theory of Personality,* $.50; and *Green Valley: A Democratic Approach to Education,* $.50; by George von Hilsheimer, Superindendent of Green Valley, Humanitas Curriculum, Orange City, Florida 32763.

appendix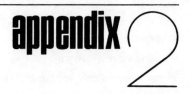

DIAGNOSTIC QUIDDITIES

In general, experience at our Humanitas facilities underlines and confirms reports which indicate that educational data is not always useful or reliable data. For example, it has been shown that two subtests on the WISC predict more reliably than the entire battery—regardless of the two subtests. It has been shown that expert psychologists can predict future behavior from case files more accurately using one or two predictors rather than the entire file. It has also been shown that many untrained individuals can evaluate appearance, behavior and language more effectively than trained individuals (if actual predictions of behavior are the criterion of effectiveness and not formal textbook categories of labelling). It has been shown that experts on behavior are about the worst single professional group in predicting actual behavior of individuals.

An entering student at our centers is given an extensive battery of evaluations. These evaluations are primarily designed to be given in such a way that the student learns to feel success in the testing situation. By experiencing success he discovers a new relationship with a teaching adult. He directly experiences perceptual and behavioral novelties. The data produced is primarily used for research and is not communicated to the staff, except in didactic ways for developing broader background insights into the processes of students in general.

However, growing out of years of experience with children in every conceivable social situation—the babies of migrants in the East Coast migrant stream, both at their Florida base and in movement; Southern rural families; big city slum children (black and Puerto Rican in New York and Chicago, sixth generation Anglo whites in Toronto); small city slum kids; middle class children both at a residential center and in their neighborhoods, and upper class and upper income children in their homes in residence at a center—we have begun to see a grouping of broad categories by which generalized responses to children can be guided.

The distinctive diagnostic categories used at Green Valley are included in this Appendix together with the specific characteristics. In general we want to find out these things about a child:

1. What is the condition of his general biological equipment? He almost surely has biological liabilities of an invasive, traumatic, ineffective, structural and objective nature.

   A. The primary dysfunctions affecting behavior that we see are:
      hypoglycemia
      allergies
      thyroid dysfunction
      dietary and metabolic deficiencies

   B. The primary functional liabilities that we see are:
      developmental lag, particularly in
         perceptual organization
      high arousal
      sleep disorder or functional narcolepsy

   C. The structural liabilities have to do with:
      physical strength
      physical dexterity and coordination
      vitality and stamina
      the reaction of these factors to stress

2. How does his nervous system handle data?

A. Measures of sympathetic nervous system activity—primarily by GSR basal levels, lability of the GSR, pupillary reflex, blood pressure, pulse rate, visceral movement; general tone and efficiency of the sympathetic system as seen in the quality of the skin, allergies and the reaction to histamine.

B. How does the person condition: Slowly, with rapid extinction, or slowly, with slow extinction; quickly, with rapid extinction or quickly, with slow extinction, etc.? A great deal can be predicted about the behavior of children in specific situations if we know their characteristic conditioning curve, their curve under stress and their curves of extinction.

C. What is the extent of cortical inhibition? This is found by discovering how the person performs on rotary pursuit tasks. Does this performance deteriorate when he is forced to do it more quickly, with a lot of distraction, or wearing prism distortion lenses? What is the characteristic tremorousness of the individual? Does he respond to stress with tremor or steadiness, increased or reduced blood pressure or pulse? What is the clinical impression: perseverance, capacity to handle boredom and immobility, capacity for detail, capacity for fine coordination? What are the discrepancies between the amount of cortical inhibition and the general performance?

D. What is the extent of physiological arousal? Almost all children referred to special classes will maintain states of high arousal for long periods of time. Does the arousal rapidly subside under instruction or suggestion? Does the arousal subside quickly with rest, moderate food, emotional support—or does it sustain despite physiological and emotional safety? What is the extent of the effect of the arousal on perception and skills?

E. What is the amount of "jam"? Does the person respond strongly to authority symbols—autonomically as well as behaviorally? What is his level of suggestibility—measured both by paper and pencil tests and sway test control versus sway test under suggestion?

F. What is the general level of performance? How consistent is it? How does it correlate with the student's basic biological equipment, motor responses, and functioning of his nervous system? A person with good strength, vitality, and motor coordination together with strong cortical inhibition, high arousal and jam, and very low achievement performance, is going to be a rough customer. A person with poor strength, low vitality, poor coordination, strong cortical inhibition, low arousal, low jam and high achievement, despite his constitutional liabilities, is going to offer little problem.

We have found that inconsistencies in the academic achievement profile are excellent predictors of behavior. High IQ/low AQ always predicts a gang-type delinquent behavior, very tough, very resilient and eventually your best product. A high AQ/low IQ always predicts a withdrawn, cooperative, inward person who presents no aggressive problems, but who is an almost unreachable passive resister. High grammar and library skills scores in children with low vocabulary and reading ranks, predict the vulnerable victim—cooperative, sweet, uncreative, a "good" formal student. Reading subtest discrepancies always go with erratic behavior and poor performance. Low scores in general predict difficulty. Discrepancies of low IQ with high creativity predict a person initially difficult in a good program, but rapidly cooperative, outgoing and productive; but if the program is that of the standard classroom, this will be the person who is most difficult, just under the high IQ gangster.

These categories let us know when isolation and close management will be therapeutic or merely managerially efficient. Individuals with low inhibition will in general benefit from well organized drill, close management, contingent reward systems, confinement, steadiness and quiet training.

In general, verbal/affective/active individuals, when strongly resistant and not suffering extreme perceptual distortion and hallucinations, will respond to very high input, including violence. In general, nonverbal/inhibited autistic/pseudoneurotic individuals will deteriorate under personal stress and must receive a great deal of support and no hint of violence.

It is ridiculous to submit low performance, low cortical inhibition, high arousal, quickly conditioning and rapidly extinguishing kids to remedial drills. They are not there to engage the material. The arousal must come down in general; this will only occur over a long period of time, with profound support, environmental change, activity, general biological strengthening and enjoyment. On the other hand, high performing kids, with high cortical inhibition, can be pushed into all kinds of drills and routines with a great deal of success.

In general, we find that untrained staff respond intuitively to children, with great accuracy. We see no evidence that anyone can be trained in accurate empathy, warmth and fairness which seem to be the only variables separating good therapists from poor therapists. The teacher will be well advised to forget diagnostic categories and allow the child to diagnose himself, by providing an elaborate choice structure in the classroom or center. Well funded centers with "medical" orientations would be well advised, however, to attend to the biological and neurological realities of the child. Not one of 222 secondary students admitted by us in five years ending June, 1968, was referred with even a basic physical inventory. Nearly half were functionally incapable of reading, almost none of whom had enjoyed any eye examination other than the most superficial. Almost all of the 222 were supplied with ten or more pages of "diagnosis"—a word which seems to mean literary speculation about the moral dynamics of the child as seen from various sectarian points of view. Untreated hypoglycemia, allergies, dietary deficiencies, thyroid dysfunctions, and narcolepsy occurred in 211 of the 222.

A teacher in any facility, regardless of its limitations, who does not do everything in her power to get a full medical inventory on a troubling child ought to turn in her certificate.

A teacher who takes any psychologist seriously ought to ask him a few questions:

1. Will this child be active in the classroom or withdrawn?
2. If pushed by the teacher will this child fight, snarl, cry, tear up and withdraw, or just withdraw?
3. Will this child enjoy play or not? Will he join in with the other kids?
4. Will this child have a lot of accidents or not?
5. Will this child be able to learn how to read? How long will it take?
6. Will this child try to harm another child or not?
7. If I lose my temper and smack this child will I lose him or not?

If you have some kids with really strange behavioral backgrounds—say a 9-12 year old murderer—ask the psychologist, "How does this child differ from the others that look and behave just like him but haven't ever harmed anyone?" "Will this child try to harm someone or himself?"

These are not questions that can be answered out of paper and pencil and consulting room experience. The best information about very distinctive behavior categories like childish murderers is that they cannot be distinguished from kids with similar social backgrounds. Delinquency and other aberrations can be predicted and simple guidelines (below) will give the teacher enough data to recommend the most reasonable therapeutic intervention—drastic change of environment, removal from home, neighborhood and school, preferably to a supportive environment with firm, clear, fair boundaries. *There is absolutely no evidence that child guidance clinics, child psychiatry or psychotherapy has any usefulness for children (or adults for that matter) at all.*

Before recommending transfer of a child to another home and neighborhood or placement in a residential school, have him evaluated by a physician who is thorough, conscientious and familiar with the behavioral consequences of apparently minor things like worms, iron deficiencies, minor allergies, vitamin B or C deficiencies, thyroid dysfunctions, sleep irregularity as well as more serious problems like hypoglycemia, extensive allergies, diabetes, narcolepsy, epilepsy and other CNS anomalies or other diseases and disorders.

Green Valley diagnostic categories:
schizophrenia
psychopath
pseudoneurotic psychopath
socially maladjusted inadequate
inhibited autistic inadequate
pseudoneurotic schizophrenic
socially disordered normal (adjustment reaction)

Diagnostic categories treated as psychopathic:
functional narcolept
affective/active homosexual
alcoholic
addict (except glue sniffers and depressive cannabis addicts)

Other important categories:
Kanner's Syndrome (Early Infantile Autism)
invasive brain trauma
excititory nonverbal brain syndrome

SCHIZOPHRENIA:

When GSR reacts it is enormously labile with very steep slopes amplitude; when the stimulus is physical (e.g., electric shock) a strong impulse is required for any reaction; then a "U" shaped response occurs—sharp drop, slow plateau, flat non-responsive phase, sharp recovery. This is also seen, in severe cases, with nonphysical stimuli.

Pupillary response tends to be minimal.

Very high basal GSR, extremely high resting GSR (ranges from 100,000 to 2,000,000 ohms).

GSR very reactive to physical motions (breathing, scratching nose, minor adjustments).

Extremely high pain threshold

194

Low or no histemic reaction
No allergies
Excellent skin
Superior healing, resistance to bruises and medical shock
Perceptual distortions
Very rapid conditioning and loss of conditioning so that conditioning does not appear to occur.
Negative reinforcement more powerful than positive. Rewards often disintegrate behavior.
Tends not to resume interrupted tasks, puzzles, etc. Being allowed to resume interrupted tasks cannot be used as an unconditional reinforcement.
Field dependent.

Pseudoneutrotic Schizophrenia
Behaviorally resemble pseudo-
    neurotic psychopaths

Affective/active Schizophrenia
Highly verbal, active
Actively expresses perceptual distortions, hallucinations
Agitated, ruminative and fearful
Frequently loses toilet training
Almost no sleep, particularly during crises
Episodic behavioral anomalies (twirling, etc.)
"Schizophrenic" physiognomy

PSYCHOPATH:
Strong histemic reaction
Physically strong
Good lung capacity
Frequent and strong allergies
Low resistance to skin staphococcus infections
Easily bruised
Females particularly are typified by bad skin, sores, cuts and bruises and scratches on legs
Slow healing
Inability to delay
Easily frustrated and regressive
If confined, satisfied with immobility
Frequently remains in own or other quarters quite immobile

Irregular sleep habits
Good coordination
High arousal
Theatrically inappropriate expression of emotion
Emotionally flat
High abstraction/generalization in all ideation
High negativity, "jam", Tom Sawyer Phenomenon
Resistant to electrical current and pain
Middle range basal GSR
Very labile GSR and puillary response
Very reactive to pain once threshold reached
Extremely slow to condition, may not condition at all

Pseudoneurotic psychopaths

High cortical inhibition
Quiet/active orderly behavior
Self-destructive
Center of social chaos (particularly in the history)
Girls often sexually hyperactive— with Lesbianic fears or behavior and total lack of satisfaction
Ruminative but not agitated
Verbally unexpressed but visibly high anxiety (dysphoria)
Disorderly/dirty, particularly in quarters, but girls may be fastidious in person
Isolated
Anti-social behavior
Bizarre clothing/hair, etc.
Passively exhibitionistic
Prefers darkness (though not necessarily in clothing)
Depressive
Easily intoxicated
1. Verbal/mystic
2. Nonverbal

Verbal/active psychopaths

Erratic cortical inhibition (high percentage of narcolepsy)
Drugs but not addicted
Well organized with episodic disintegration usually associated with drugs
Charming/social, or at least surface friendly
Strong, active, destructive social behavior fairly constant
Frequently good athletes, but with characteristic clumsiness combined with formally high coordination and skill
Boys and girls constant bi-sexual hyperactive unsatisfying sexuality
Exhibitionisitic

INADEQUATE PERSONALITIES

Physically weak
Small lung capacity
Easily tired
Developmental lag
Perceptually immature
Frequently sick and hypochondriac
Strong reaction to histamine
Frequent and strong allergies
Low resistance to skin staph infection
Easily bruised
Slow healers
Strong medical shock
Easily agitated
Stressed by immobility
Poor coordination
Easily frustrated with infantile regression
Poor emotional control, tearful, raging
Low cortical inhibition
Tremorous
High Arousal
High Field Dependence
Extremely manipulable
Low pain threshold
Very reactive pupil and GSR
Very low basal GSR
Very fast conditioning
Very fast extinction of conditioning

Socially maladjusted inadequate

"Loser" criminals
Usually self mutilated, tattooed
Sloppy and unattractive
Extremely verbal
Inattentatively verbal
Repetitiously verbal with gross generalized distortions
Self pitying
Super malingerers
Low IQ
Easily intoxicated, out of control when intoxicated

Inhibited/autistic inadequate

Isolated
Frequently jowly, and acned (esp. girls)
Downcast eyes (esp. girls)
Dislikes red, red can be used as a negative reinforcement or punishment
Withdrawn cooperative
Easily intoxicated
Self pitying
Very nonverbal
Often "twitchy"
Erratic cortical inhibition
Sometimes high IQ

SUCCESS SIGNS

Reliable predictors of reeducation success and ease of reeducation in residence as seen in 222 secondary age students.

High IQ
High arithmetic ability
High reading ability
High achievement test rank
Low IQ/arithmetic discrepancy
Low IQ/achievement discrepancy
Smooth achievement profile
Low vocabulary/grammar discrepancy
Low vocabulary/math discrepancy
Low vocabulary/reading discrepancy
Low reading test/low reading ability discrepancy
Former grades (initial grades after discharge)
Low authoritarian (Adorno/Rokeach) score
Low discrepancy on Q-sorts of ideal and perceived self images
Moderate "normal" reaction on sway suggestion test
Low score on Glover Inventory of Sexual Values
Low field dependence (males)
Ready perception of the Ames Rotating Window Illusion; the
    Necker Cube and Necker Star Rotating Illusions
High coordination and perserverance on a rotary pursuit task
Low discrepancy on coordination control/coordination under
    stress
Low hand tremor
Low discrepancy hand tremor control/hand tremor under stress
Health record in residence

SUCCESS SIGNS *(continued)*

STAFF/STUDENT EVALUATIONS:
Structured resistance to authority as opposed to undifferentiated resistance or slavish obedience
Articulate self-description
Articulate world view
Good appearance
Good grooming and housekeeping
Perseverance at boring work
Independent work discipline
College or work goal clearly articulated
Competent engagement in school meetings
Peer rank
Staff rank
Low peer/staff rank discrepancy

Normalization of Biological Variables

appendix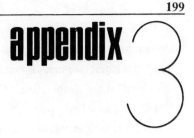

DANGER SIGNS

Signalling need for medical inventory, closer management, and radical environmental change.

1. Sleep irregularities, particularly sudden loss of sleep rhythm, extensive sleeplessness often coupled with very heavy morning and daytime sleep.

2. Irritability, raging, loss of control, sullenness.

3. Rapid changes in mood.

4. Sudden and clear changes in behavior, regression to earlier patterns of behavior. (Did the child ever suddenly refuse to talk after learning to do so?)

5. Withdrawal from other children.

6. Setting fires (particularly if combined with bed wetting).

7. Lack of humor.

8. Destructiveness, cruelty. Lots of verbal "killing," particularly parents.

9. Blinking—particularly slow sleepy blinks paired with rapid bursts of blinking under stress, when lying, etc.

10. Tics, nail-biting, worrying, nibbling, nervousness and restlessness, drivenness, short attention span, poor concentration.

12. Regressive, tearing but not crying, over sensitivity to criticism, "martyr" complex.

12. Tom Sawyer phenomenon to an unusual extent—disregard and defiance of punishment, self-mutilation, pain fascination, "Jam."

13. Extreme superman complex, preoccupation with guns and knives and other destructive utensils.

14. Dislike of and poor performance in school, particularly discrepancies in achievement/ability, *and most particularly, poor reading.*

15. Truancy.

If, in addition, the father's ways of disciplining the child are overstrict or completely laissez faire; the mother's supervision is poor, erratic, overstrict, or absent; the father is indifferent or hostile to the child; the mother is indifferent or hostile to the child; if either parent is absent; or the family is unintegrated, disruptive, argumentative, or erratic; then the child is most likely to become delinquent, or otherwise aberrant.

Our experience with more than 500 difficult children indicates that about the worst thing that can happen to a potentially difficult boy is to be raised by his mother, or to be in a home with a dominant mother. (It doesn't much matter whether the domination is by hysteria, neurosis or rigidly integrated strength, given the predisposition of the child.) Nearly all of our children come from homes with mother liabilities. A strong, warm woman, capable of maintaining integrity of the home structure can offset the absence, laxity, or overstrictness and indifference or hostility of the father. To some extent this seems true for fathers—but the logistics are difficult for fathers. If you drew a weak or angry mother you just seem to have had it. The offsetting abilities of fathers seem reduced as you go up the income scale, which probably reflects the reduced home life of executives, managers and other high income professionals.

We emphasize, however, that our population of about 500 secondary age children reveal only about 125 children who we are thoroughly convinced were primarily disordred because of the home and parents. Parents may be unable to cope with behavior caused by other factors, and may exacerbate the problems by the quality of their responsiveness. We have seen many children from homes with other children who are perfectly well off, productive and well behaved. Teachers should remember that no population, no matter how distorted socially, produces all problem individuals. Moreover, no population, no matter how socially ideal, produces no problem individuals. It is our belief that we can best be of service to the child by focusing on him as an individual in his peer society. If he can function satisfactorily in both the society of his peers and toward the artificial demands of school, he will very likely survive intact.

Our research has thoroughly convinced us that as long as the child is manageable in the school without drastic tactics, the best thing the teacher can do for him is to teach him to read and write and to enjoy it. Nothing in the literature reveals a more therapeutic intervention. If the teacher becomes convinced that she simply cannot teach a specific child those fundamental skills within the limitations of her classroom and school, then, and only then should she fight to have him in a new environment.

appendix 4

SOURCES OF MATERIALS AND DEVICES

ITEMS & DESCRIPTION:	*ORDER FROM:*
CUISENAIRE RODS (color coded rods beginning with cube for one, going through ten, each a different color)	CUISENAIRE COMPANY OF AMERICA 9 Elm Avenue Mt. Vernon, New York 10550
MASTER CUBE (set of scored cubes & rectangles making several figures and a system for algebraic instructions)	AMERICAN PRINTING HOUSE FOR THE BLIND 1839 Frankfort Avenue Louisville, Kentucky 40206
MITCHELL WIRE FORMS (set of large geometric figures, with matching sets of solid and open forms matching the planes of the solids)	SAME
ABAMAT (a modern abacus with color coded beads for multiplying and dividing; text uses "the first abacus" system introducing the abacus from a finger system)	HUMANITAS Monastery Road Orange City, Florida 32763
HOW MANY? (semi-programmed new math primer in color book form)	SAME
BASIC ENGLISH (one page listing of the basic 800 words necessary to communicate in English)	SAME

ITEMS & DESCRIPTION (Continued)

ROTATING ILLUSION, Model PT 12 (includes Ames window and a Neckar cube and a Neckar star)	RESEARCH MEDIA, INC. 163 Eileen Way Syossett, Long Island, N.Y. 11791
AMES ROOM ILLUSION	SAME

GEOMETRIC FORMS

Set of 27 basic solids (about 5/8") in plastic (No. 60,249)

Set of equal volume solids (1" cube) (No. 60,250)

Set of large transparent solids (No. 70,314)

Set of cut-outs on card stock to form solids (No. 9,062)

100 (1") colored wooden cubes (No. 70,332)

125 (1") wooden cubes color coded to show cubes-in-cubes (No. 90,056)

12 Wooden Puzzles (No. 70,205)

Soma Wood Block Puzzle (No. 70,265)

28 Large Wooden Dominoes (No. 90,020)

"Think Sticks" (1/8") birch sticks with connectors (452 pieces) (No. 70,211)

EDMUND SCIENTIFIC
600 Edscorp Bldg.
Barrington, New Jersey
08007

"SHOCK BOX"—Model 100—supplies with ring electrodes—battery operated

HUMANITAS SYSTEMS
Rt. 2
Roscoe, N.Y. 12776

"TINKLE BELL"—Model 200—Urination Alarm

SAME

"MOTION SENSOR"—Model 300

SAME

GALVANIC SKIN RESPONSE METER— Model 500 GSR

SAME

THE BLINKY BOX—Model 900—Stimulus

SAME

CONDITIONING APPARATUS—Model 1000—Inhibitron

SAME

MODERN READING

HUMANITAS
Curriculum Publications
Box 606
Orange City, Florida 32763

ITEMS & DESCRIPTION (*Continued*)

PROGRAMMED READING ABILITY   SAME
  PRESCHOOL

THREE MINUTE LANGUAGE   SAME
  SYSTEMS
    Hebrew
    Spanish

35mm SLIDES   SAME
  Authority
  Death
  Dirt
  Exhibition
  Distortion
  Affection
  Aggression
  Mothers
  Homosexuality (Male or Female)
  Paedophilia (Male)

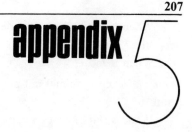

appendix

A THOUSAND AND ONE LESSON PLANS

Identities

Who am I?

Human. How do I tell the difference between human and non-human?

White, black, yellow, brown. All human?

Man, gorilla, chimpanzee, orangutan, gibbon, Old World monkey, New World monkey, lemur.

Is man more different from a chimp than an embryonic man? fetus? baby? pig?

How do I tell a robot to tell the difference between:
    man/ embryonicman/ fetalman/ babyman/ childman and
    gorilla, chimp, orangutan, etc.
    pig/ embryonicpig/ fetalpig/ babypig/ childpig/
    fish/ embryonicfish
    humanoid robot

Alive. How do I tell the difference between alive and not alive?

colloidal jelly, jellyfish, self-reproducing machine (demonstrate one), virus, crystal, amorphous mass, gas, star, stone, computer, adding machine, analog computer, ballistic missile, self-guided missile, dummy, dolphin, whale, mongoloid, anomalous subidiot.

Why do we eat whales and dolphins and not idiots?

When is dead? Why do a dead man's heart, liver, kidney, eyes, teeth live?

When is meat?

Animal. When is animal not plant? Does a cabbage feel? Do animals think?

What is think? Does a computer think? Will one?

Is think always think? Do people think? Most people? Some? What is rational/irrational?

Do pigs hurt?

Smart. What is smart? How is dumb? Can a dog talk? Can it write poetry? Can a pig learn to take a shower? Can a fish learn to dance?

Is "fast/almost accurate" smarter than "slow/always accurate?"

Is "always remembers" smarter than "figures things out?"

Individual. How is one an individual? Where do you begin and I leave off? When are you separated from your parents?

Is a hawk chasing a bird separate from the bird?

Can you, without touching me, make changes in me that I can't make?

Well, why don't you listen to me tell you to imagine sliding down a 10 foot razor blade—can you make yourself feel that way?

If Nice Person tells you "I love you" can you make yourself feel the same way without Nice Person?

If Wanted Person says "I hate you" can you make yourself feel the same way? Can you put yourself back together again?

When a foot pushes an accelerator is it different than when a leg pushes a foot? How?

Is a telephone me? A telescope? An artificial arm? A transplanted heart?

Am I different when I am with six people? One other? Myself in a closet? Boys? Girls? Men? Women? Crowds? Sitting quietly? Playing a game? Fighting? Loving? Hating?

If everybody looks at you, where are you?

Where are you when you are asleep? Just very sleepy? What if half your brain is gone? Fever? Drugs? No vitamin B—pellagra?

THINGS TO DO

Go up into a high building. Look down.

What are people doing? Where are they going?

What happened to the air?

Who pays for the smoke?

Which way are the cars going?

How much space do the roads take?

Where is the green?

Where is work?

How does traffic move?

What goes on where? Particularly at night?

Drive in the country.

How big are the trees?

Are they different? Different sizes? Are most about the same? Why might that be?

What were the fields? How many farmers were there?

How do farmers know each other?

What does a church do?

What does a bar do?

What does a store do?

Where are people?

Who works, where do they live? Who picks things up?

Look around the school.

Who is the janitor?

Where does food come from? where kept? who fixes? what do they do all day? who are they?

How are walls clean?

How is a school used? No, *really?*

How much wall is there? What is a wall? What does it do?

What are spaces for?

What does the school do most of the time?

How much does it do?

Does the school have a yard? *Really?*

What does the yard do? How does it do with students?

Design a school—do it all over again. Make one for people like the Zulu s who can't make or see straight lines.

Design a neighborhood.

Design a city.

Design a hospital with no walls.

What is walk? Is run walk?

If you had a pencil sticking straight out of a car tire what kind of line would it draw on paper? What is roll? What is a wheel?

Is there a figure that has the same diameter from every point to every point opposite and isn't a circle (clue: there is)?

What is a child?

appendix 6

A FOUR WEEK REMEDIAL READING PROGRAM FOR 8-12 YEAR OLD BOYS

by
Hulda R. Clark, Ph.D.

Designed to produce one year's progress in reading skills

GOAL: One school-year advancement in reading ability.

PUPILS: Boys, age 8-12, with grade 1 reading ability.

TIME: 1/2-1 hour daily. Actual total teaching time per pupil 200 minutes.

SPECIAL CLASSWORK: None related to reading.

SETTING: Classroom with desks shoved to one end. Cleared area for "belly-reading" on floor has shelves containing these comic books:

> Casper
> Tom & Jerry
> Hot Stuff
> Wendy The Witch
> Woody Woodpecker

TEACHER & ASSISTANT: Both male, if available.

SIZE OF CLASS: Recommend 6—upper limit set by teacher—noise, discipline.

WEEK NO. 1

DAY NO. 1:

Teacher: "Boys, which would you rather read, Story Books or Comic Books?"

Answer: "Comic Books!"

Teacher: O.K. Get Busy. You can read down on the floor if you want to. When you're done come up here and tell me which ones you read."

Note: Do not ask "how much did you read." Also, if possible, avoid setting a time requirement. If a pupil "is done" in less than 15 minutes suggest to him, "Go read another one; pick a harder one this time."

Expect child to read one comic story—not entire book. Allow gum-chewing or distribute gum if feasible. Do not check up on portions skipped, words not read, or poor comprehension. However, try to avoid blatant cheating by page-skipping.

Pupils will read only about 1/10 of words on first reading. Let pupils go after 20 minutes. Keep the atmosphere humorous and friendly. Permit conversation and loud reading and dramatization if not too lengthy and if feasible.

COMMENT TO EACH CHILD as he reports his reading to you, "That's GOOD."

DAY NO. 2:

Teacher: Pass out the gum. Wait 5-10 minutes to permit pupils to settle down to reading by themselves, if capable. Then announce: "Boys, you may read the same book as yesterday if you want to. Come up and show me what you read when you're done. You can ask me for a word if you can't get it." Again, permit social conversation if not too lengthy. Permit loud reading—separate the loud readers. Do not check on poor reading habits—lip moves, voicing, finger following.

Again do not test child for comprehension, words skipped, etc.

Note: If a pupil asks teacher's help about a word, do not explain HOW to read it, or HOW to sound it out. Simply tell the word, and *then* as a bonus, read a few extra squares, dramatically and with humor, to set precedent of style in reading.

DAY NO. 3-5:

Permit and encourage choice of the same book. Suggest reading the entire book minus the fine-print stories.

PRAISE EACH CHILD INDIVIDUALLY.

EXPECTED RESULTS AFTER FIRST WEEK:

1. ENJOYMENT of "Reading hour"
2. Familiarity with variety of comic books
3. Acquisition of simplest "comic" vocabulary

WEEK NO. 2

DAYS NO. 1-5:

Pass gum. Wait 5-10 minutes for boys to socialize and to permit those pupils with initiative to make their own choice of comics or books. Then quietly help the remainder individually to make a choice.

Do not state a time requirement but attempt to maintain a minimum of 1/2 hour of actual reading time per child. Encourage longer stay.

EXPECTED RESULTS AFTER SECOND WEEK:

1. Less goofing and self-interruptions
2. Better concentration despite noise, etc.
3. Longer attention span
4. Better mastery of simple "comic" vocabulary
5. Increased interest in reading a variety of comic books

WEEK NO. 3

DAY NO. 1:

(20 minute reading lesson) Pass out the gum. Wait about 5 minutes for pupils to exercise initiative in reading. Now

choose one pupil who is still at large and call him to teacher's desk.

Teacher: "I'm going to time you with the stop watch. Which book do you want to read, 'Duck on the Truck' or 'Sam and the Firefly?' Take your choice—O.K.!" Teacher sits *across* from the child, close enough to read upside down. Place wristwatch or stopwatch on desk—time completion of the book.

NOW, teacher gets child started by placing finger above each word as TEACHER reads loudly. If child does not join in, say "Read with me."

If the child is able to carry on by himself briefly teacher drops out for a line or a few words, then joining in again briefly. TEACHER READS MOST OF THE WORDS. Do not select difficult words for helping. Do not permit hesitation or dawdling or prolonged word sounding. Read along swiftly in order to keep the child's eyes trained *on the word being read.* Watch pupil's eyes closely. If pupil gazes at the picture, do the same. Do not ask him if he is ready. Say "Let's go now" and cover picture with hand.

Do not emphasize comprehension in first reading, nor test him on any aspect of it. Do not distract child with comments on posture or on habits (e.g., get yourself a Kleenex). AVOID BEING INTERRUPTED. Cover at least 20 pages in first reading session; if possible, the whole book. COMMENT: "VERY GOOD! YOU GOT TO PAGE 21. That took 10 minutes and 22 seconds." Then allow child to join comic readers. Accept volunteers by preference.

DAY NO. 2 (20 minute reading lesson):

Teacher asks at once "Who wants to read first?" Encourage volunteering if practical.

Choose *same book* as yesterday. Begin at the beginning! Get pupil started as before, to set the pace and to give a tone of drama and humor. Take time to act out and gesticulate, and to repeat an especially dramatic line. Read loudly!

Teacher reads about 1/2 the words, without selecting only the difficult passages. *Avoid all interruptions.* Attempt to read 30 pages.

DAY NO. 3 (20 minute reading lesson):

Request pupil to "Find your book." Wait a few minutes to permit child to begin on his own (silent or aloud) if so inclined.

Then Teacher: "How far are you?"
Pupil: "Up to here."
Teacher: "Good going."

Begin at once to read aloud, together, as before, continuing from where the child indicated. Read rapidly leaving most of the words for the child to read. Join in on hesitations even if this includes very simple words such as *in, out, for, by.* After several minutes, take leave of the child to tend to some other chore, still observing whether he continues alone, silently or aloud.

Upon returning, ask "how far are you?" Do not reprimand child for taking "time out" in your absence.

Now read swiftly together to end of book, if possible, in the twenty minutes allowed. COMMENT TO CHILD— "YOU DID VERY WELL TODAY."

DAY NO. 4:

Same book. Follow same procedure as for Day No. 3, *except* when taking the brief leave of absence, say "You read the next few pages." Do not test the child on whether your instructions were carried out. At end, PRAISE CHILD and permit him to read comic books as usual.

DAY NO. 5:

Same book. Same procedure, except when taking leave of absence say "You may read to yourself, if you want to" or "you may read quietly, if you want to." Record the time taken to finish book.

EXPECTED RESULTS AFTER THIRD WEEK:

1. Mastery of simplest Grade 1 vocabulary, such as *in, by, of, out.*
2. Good attention span.
3. Reading with dramatic voice.
4. Good speed, with help.

WEEK NO. 4

DAY NO. 1 (15-20 minute lesson):

> Begin by suggesting: "Let's beat that 22 minutes and 10 seconds today."
>
> Get the child started, setting a rapid pace, using finger motion to help slower ones track properly. Contribute whenever necessary. Make the drama hilarious but speedy. Do not leave the child during lesson. Record his time. *PRAISE. Avoid all interruption.* If child absolutely cannot be kept interested in same choice of book, permit him to start on "Sam and the Firefly" one day early.

DAY NO. 2 (15-20 minute lesson):

Teacher: "You may read 'Sam and the Firefly' today."

> Get the child started, quite rapidly, contributing about 1/2 the words. Use finger-tracking to assure that the child's eyes are *on the word being spoken.* Read 1/2 the book. *Avoid any interruptions.*

DAY NO. 3 (15-20 minute lesson):

> Read from beginning and attempt to finish book. Do not check on comprehension. Emphasize speed. *Avoid interruptions.* Record his time on back of book.

DAY NO. 4:

> Let child read alone, silently, if he performs adequately. After about 10 minutes of silent reading, join in, reading aloud as usual to the end. Emphasize drama and humor.

DAY NO. 5 (15-20 minutes lesson):

> Record time to read entire book, contributing frequently and swiftly as needed. *Avoid all interruptions.* PRAISE CHILD.

> EXPECTED RESULTS AFTER FOURTH WEEK:
> 1. Reading achievement—2nd grade level
> 2. Improved behavior
> 3. Improved arithmetic grades
> 4. Improved concentration and comprehension.

This program may be continued, of course, if more reading progress is desired. To achieve 3rd grade level, another four weeks of intensive 20 minute lessons are required, covering 4 additional 50 page books. Again no explanatory teaching is done. Emphasis is on drama and speed. An important goal throughout is to eliminate dawdling.

appendix 7

TIPS FOR TEENAGE VOLUNTEERS WITH YOUNG CHILDREN IN THE CLASSROOM

Hulda R. Clark, Ph.D.

WHY ARE YOU CHOSEN?

Because YOU are such a special person just naturally better suited to the job than an adult is.

Of course this means: Don't try to act like an adult (that is, a teacher or parent) because you would lose this special effectiveness you have as a teenager—just being yourself.

BREAKING THE ICE

Children know just how it feels to be new. It happens to them so often. So you don't have to be smooth and talkative right away.

It isn't really important either to be introduced or to get their attention right away. Be sure to use your first name (not Mr. or Miss) so as not to seem like an adult. Just getting down to business with the project for the day will break the ice most quickly and easily.

YOU DON'T HAVE TO BE A PSYCHOLOGIST

What counts most is your FAIRNESS and your RESPECT FOR CHILDREN not "liking kids" or understanding their psychology. So just let yourself go. Sometimes you're irritable, sometimes you're impatient. You don't like every child the same amount. You're more patient with some. But it's your Fairness and Respect that do count and need your concentration. These two things go farther than all the other "good" traits. If you have Fairness and Respect it's worth more than any training or degree.

Exactly what is Fairness made of? Well, it doesn't mean treating every child the same. It means only that you give all the same justice. I mean the same kind of justice you can remember always wanting for yourself and still want now and always will want.

This means, don't listen to anybody's tattle-tale. That is, listen, but don't draw any conclusions. And after listening, assume a child is NOT GUILTY unless YOU can prove he is. That means YOU must actually SEE a child hitting or pinching or stealing or spitting or kicking in order to ACCUSE him of it. You must actually HEAR the child say the bad word or his lie to ACCUSE him of it. Nobody's tattle-tale or complaint, or the child's own guilty looking face or poor excuse, are sufficient for you to ACCUSE him.

Granted, this means a lot of kids will be getting away with a lot of things they're guilty of. And you may get that sinking feeling that you're not able to control the discipline that is your responsibility too. Yet, this is much better than accusing an innocent person even ONCE.

This kind of absolutely fair justice is more than a parent and most teachers are able to practice, though, of course, they expect it for themselves. Consequently, you are giving your children their first experience in TRUE FAIRNESS OR JUSTICE.

Now what about RESPECT? What is respect made of? It's believing that each child is worthwhile, and important. Sometimes it's very difficult to take this view, especially if there is a child or two you don't like. To conquer this feeling try to picture yourself ten years older; "your" children will be about the same age you are now. If they should run into you by chance would you be proud to have once taught them? Would they now have the respect for you that you once gave to them? As sure as rain and sunshine, the respect you give now to every single child, especially your least favorite, will be returned to you some day. So when your supply of FAIRNESS and RESPECT runs low for a few children, SIT BACK and THINK about the ten years from now.

NEVER SAY "YOU ARE . . ."

Such as:

"You are so naughty today."
"You are so happy today."
"You're messy."
"You're neat."
"You have a good imagination" meaning
     "You are imaginative."
"You are a thoughtless boy."
"You're silly."
"You're a big boy now."
"You're too old for that."
"He's just a little boy."
"What makes you such a bully?"

This is exactly how parents and teachers make children angry—so angry that they get the most horrible and bloody thoughts—maybe all sweetly concealed. Or just showing a bit through "acting up." This explains how a kid can arrive in your class, active and full of worthwhile ideas. Since you appreciate this, you'd like to keep it going all morning or afternoon, so you say "My, you are a cheerful one today." And in about one half hour the same kid seems broody and changed. Why? After all, you said a nice thing! The answer is that it's never a nice thing to say something about a child's character, either good or bad. Say all you wish about a child's actions or words but YOU MUST NOT LABEL HIS CHARACTER. His deep-inside character is his sacred personal property.

You may say:

"You've got a big mess there."
"You didn't have to hit her."

"You did a lovely job."

"Why did you do such a bad thing?"

That's entirely different from phrasing it the "You are" way. Just sticking to this one rule will make you near and dear to the hearts of your children. At home, you'd be surprised to know how much character-defamation these children have to take. They get called Dumb, Stupid, Slow-Poke, Clumsy, Deaf, Scatter-Brain, Ne'er-Do-Well, Mess Pot, Fool, Big Baby, Goose, Brainy, Old Slop and hundreds more. A parent will walk all over his own child's personal character as if it were a cheap rug. And the child gets a Big Mad Mountain growing inside of him that just gets taller and taller. Think of it this way. Having a messy bedroom doesn't mean you're messy through and through. Naturally you may be quite neat in other things, so why should you be called "The Mess Pot of the family" or "A Born Mess?" This kind of defamation lingers inside much longer than being screamed at "Your bedroom is an unholy mess," or, "Go clean up that mess of a place you call a bedroom," or, "Your room is messy, I want you to keep the door shut from now on." Of course, you might not exactly enjoy this criticism either, but at least the hurt isn't deep down and doesn't BRAND YOU.

In the same way, sharing your chocolate bar doesn't make you generous through and through. You may know yourself deep down as a long way off from being totally generous and it isn't a bit satisfying to see how easily somebody is fooled by it. Now this is what upset the cheerful mood of the child way back in the beginning when you said, "My, but you're a cheerful one today." The child may not consider himself deep down as a "cheerful one." Such a comment is both untruthful and in very poor taste. Besides, knowing how changeable young children are, your "cheerful one" might have had a bad temper just minutes before he arrived. To sum up, once more, never say:

"You're a pest."

"You have a wonderful imagination."

"You're my sunshine."

"How's my sugar 'n spice today?"

"Don't be a droopy-drawers."

"You're such a big girl."

Change all these comments into descriptions:

"You're bothering everybody."

"This shows wonderful imagination."

"Your pants are droopy."

"Wipe your nose."

THE THREE BIG RULES:

1. HELP AS LITTLE AS POSSIBLE
2. DON'T BE THE SLAVE
3. TALK, TALK, TALK

Rule Number One: Help as little as possible. Many children come from homes where even the simple things are done for them. When they were babies they were lifted into their high chairs or into the car instead of being allowed to climb in. They were carried or ridden or driven because nobody had patience to let them walk, even when they were "out for a walk." So now they expect it, holding up their arms and holding out their feet from the habit of being helped. This was never done by Chippewa Indians to their children. When father went out for a walk he didn't throw Three-Year-Old up on his shoulders. No. Three-Year-Old came straggling along on his own powerful little legs and when he stopped to climb a tree or swing a vine, father (even sister or brother) stopped too, lighting up a cigarette or leaning against a tree, with never a word like "Hurry up" or "If you don't hurry I'll leave you here." And Chippewa youngsters are as happy and playful as puppies as they swim, climb, run and jump with unbelievable agility and self-confidence. No one has ever insulted them with unwanted help.

Our children have very little self-confidence. They have lost the initiative to do things for themselves and by themselves. They think the world belongs to others, the giants (adults of all description) and they feel like little ants, just trying to get along somehow. You can give them their first feeling of bigness, strength, and importance.

Once you get them started, they will carry on alone. But how do you do this? You can't just say "Do it yourself." It simply won't work because the age for this has passed. So, when a child asks for help you say YES. What he doesn't know is that you plan to desert in less than a minute. Sometimes most of the things children want help with even seem "put on" because they're so simple, like pouring water, getting something off a shelf, holding down a piece of paper, or picking up a hammer. Don't try to embarrass him about his helplessness. Hold the cup while he pours, give him a booster while he reaches for things, put your hand over his while he squeezes the glue bottle, put his hand on the hammer handle, hold a nail for two or three blows. But then SKIP OUT, DESERT. It won't seem like heartless desertion if you're going to help another child or are busy on your own project. Don't give up. It is difficult for children to lose their helplessness by the time they're 5 years old.

For the same reasons, it isn't fair for the more confident children to help the rest. It's just common respect for everyone to let others try things and do things themselves, and make mistakes without having to accept help or advice.

But what if there's just one big chorus of ten or more voices squealing at you "I can't," "I don't know how," "You do it," or "Show me," until you don't know what to do or think? If it's just not your day to cope with it you can say, "Do something else, then." You'll know you have succeeded when you hardly ever get asked for help any more. And you have enough time to go around offering help here and there. It may take a half a year to accomplish this. But remember it took four or five years to make the child so helpless. If you can give him back his courage in half a year you have done a great deal. So remember: always say YES to a call for help, get it started and then SKIP OUT.

Rule Number Two: Don't be the slave. Being enslaved is quite different from being helpful. Children will try to enslave you to put you in their power, not because they want help. This rule comes naturally to you at home or with your friends. But when you're with little children you might be tempted to make a servant of yourself as mothers often do. DON'T. Many children have been raised by parents who try to keep their children away from pain, away from anxiety, away from anger, away from failures, away from everything negative in life, and accomplish this by subterfuge, deception and enslavement of the whole family. You can be kind, be interested, be sympathetic, but don't be A SLAVE MOTHER. Say "There's the fountain, go get yourself a drink," "There's the boy's washroom, just push the door hard," "Take your own coat off," "Zip up your jacket before you go out," "I see it. It's a sliver. See if you can get it out with a needle or ask your dad to do it," "Get yourself a bandaid." DON'T BE A MOTHER means more than this. Don't say in a snide little way, "Now I wonder who could have left his jacket here on the floor!", "I think you forgot to say something"; "Now really." I don't have to add that there are quite a few more "mothery" things that you just hated, and maybe still have to put up with. So pay close attention to omitting them from your behavior.

Rule Number Three: Talk, Talk, Talk. Not just these children, all children are still raised to be seen and not heard. Oh, they'll be heard all right if they're feeling sweet, sunshiny, considerate, patient and mannerly and mother feels up to responding. But a child knows when to stop. If it makes mother or dad worried and get a funny tense look on their faces, or worse yet if mother acts shocked to hear such a thing or question, that's the clue to drop the subject, often forever. Now you have the unique opportunity to give these children a hearing. Sure, they can talk about and ask about things to their friends or brothers and sisters. But these answers don't help them enough. They want better answers. Your answers. You'll see what I mean. Suppose you're telling little David how you put out fire with water on a camping trip and little Marsha speaks up, "I caughted on fire once. Johnny, that's my brother, he lighted me with a match." You say, "Did you know what to do then? Did you lie down and roll it out?" "No, Johnny putted it out." You say, "Gee, didn't your mother get mad?" "Johnny smeared mud all over it and I put it in the laundry." "What if your mother asks who burned that hole, are you going to lie or tell on Johnny?" "I'm gonna say a dog bit me." "Do you like Johnny?" "He told me to say that." "If you don't tell, he might burn somebody else, or your house and your baby." "Well, we have fire insurance." "How do you know?" "Johnny said." "That doesn't mean you get everything back, your house and your baby and all your dad's stuff and everything." "Ohhhhhh!" In this conversation, you may have helped Marsha find her courage. Nobody else could.

What if the children just don't seem to open up to you, just can't get talking freely somehow. TRY HUMOR. What is sure to tickle a four or five year old? DRAMATICS AND FUNNY WORDS. What are dramatics? "Here's how a pussy cat drinks milk." "Here's a monkey walking down the street." If this isn't exactly your cup of tea, try funny words. Like "Bass the burple baint, please." for "Pass the purple paint, please." Or "Here's the hammer wammer." A laughing session is well worth the time spent on it. After a laughing-bee, the children often feel "on the inside" with you, a family-like feeling. You're likely to hear some deeper darker secrets after these times, like "Henry pee-ed outside once," or "John said the F-word on the school yard once," or "My brother tried to marry Rover. Rover's a black dog." What should you say? It's a precious moment. If you look shocked or pretend you don't hear or just don't answer—well, then you've chickened out like the parents would. Be ready with two stock answers for those times when you get surprise questions like "Do you kiss?" or "Do you believe babies are born out of—you know where— butts?" Say "I suppose so" until you can collect your wits. Saying "I suppose so" never spoils anything and gets you safely past the shock period. Kids hate to upset you and then have to face you about it. But once the shock is past, what do you really answer?

You're pretty well on your own here and if the parents don't object, I would simply recommend telling the plain truth. Like "Santa Claus is really your dad dressed up." "Babies don't come out of the pee-hole, they come out beside the pee-hole." But just keep it simple, talking while you're working. Don't worry about making mistakes.

The children don't mind if you go into reverse on something. For example, if you originally said, "You kill a dog when he's old and sick so he won't suffer any more" and now prefer a different answer, it's quite all right to turn about and say, "I wouldn't kill a dog if he was old and sick. I forgot that old and sick dogs are important for scientific experiments. I'd call up the hospital and see if they need him." If some questions simply stump you completely, say, "You'll find out someday. When you're old enough to read books you can find out for yourself; you can find every, every, everything in some book, even with pictures."

WHAT ABOUT FIGHTING OR SCRAPPING OR BEING UNFAIR?

For instance, grabbing stuff. Girls especially, grab stuff away from boys because boys can't retaliate well. If possible, don't see it. Only step in and arbitrate if necessary. First listen to who started it, and who used an unfair punch and to the whole story. Then say, "Well, there's another thing to do, you know. You could get yourself a different one, or you could wait till he's done, or. . . ." Minimize trouble or apply humor where possible. Suppose the girl now throws him the tool or glue or whatever they were fighting over, saying, "Here, baby." Just don't pay any more attention. Let trouble lie.

Not every conflict has to be resolved. Children can be encouraged to "give" or "yield." But to put a ban on fighting and scrapping, merely pushes the conflict outside your four walls. It would be more helpful to stage a real contest with rules of fairness that the child could take with him into the world.

THE REAL HAZARDS

Slippery shoes on a slippery floor are the worst hazard. Let the children go barefoot if the parents won't get them rubber soled shoes. Falling causes most accidents. Pushing a stick ahead of him. Carrying something in his mouth. Sucking on a marble. One little toy wheel on an axle, lying on the floor. These are more dangerous than using knives and scissors.

THE LAST LITTLE TRUTHS

1. Don't worry the parent. This means don't talk to the parent about his child's problems or negative behavior. That's your secret. WHY? Because junior will find out—even just sense—that you "talked" about him. And from then on you are a deceptive cheater in his book. Anyway, telling parents never improves things.

2. You can't be perfect. The world is full of mistakes and you're bound to add to the pile sometimes. So just live them down.

3. Don't quit when you're down. Sleep on your problem. Then in the cold light of day chisel out a decision you can be proud of. FOR YOUR CHILDREN'S SAKE always.

Good Luck,

Hulda R. Clark, Ph.D.

appendix 8

THE GREEN VALLEY TEST SERIES
AND
ORGANIZATION FOR REDUCTION OF TEST BLOCK

Every entering student devotes his first three months to morning and afternoon sessions of testing—60 school days in all. There are three main purposes for these tests:

First: to give the student completely novel experiences, called "Testing" in which he must learn and must succeed and so break up his habit of failure;

Second: to give the staff detailed, objective, quantified data about the student's physical and motor capacities and organization, about the way in which he perceptually deals with the world around him and senses his internal processes, and his intellectual capacities and performances as well as his specific academic performance;

Third: to carry out research evaluating standard methods of testing, and creating new means of objectively describing and predicting the dynamics of the behavior of adolescents and young adults.

1. The student is confronted with the AMES WINDOW illusion, the NECKAR CUBE, and the NECKAR STAR. Both the quantity of illusions perceived, and the time required for perception give information about physiological arousal, cortical inhibition, and gestalt forming abilities.

2. ROGER'S Estimate the Number of Dots Cards are displayed in sequences to the students. Both his ability to quantify displays and his ability to learn simple tasks are measured.

3. In a number of sessions the student is asked to describe, and then organize at will large geometric forms and their planes as represented by flat wooden surfaces and wire forms, then very small plastic solid forms and then rods and connectors.

4. The student is asked to construct anything he wants using CUISENAIRE RODS and then again using rods varying from a one inch cube to a one inch by one inch by twelve inch rod.

5. The student is tested on a rotary pursuit apparatus. This performance is compared under the stress of performing while wearing lenses distorting vision fifteen degrees.

6. An exploded four inch cube is presented to the student to assemble. The time to assemble the MASTER CUBE correlates well with both verbal and motor intelligence.

7. A box of geometrical forms can be replaced only through holes corresponding to their exact shape. The time and retime required to sort correlates well with intelligence.

8. Doughnut disks are placed as rapidly as possible on a series of dowels that will hold from one to ten of the disks. Time and retime.

9. Hand tremor is measured with and without distortion lenses.

10. The student is required to switch, using both hands, controls operating a bell, buzzer and tone to tape recorded verbal commands, to signal commands, matching the sound, and to visual commands by light flashes.

11. ROD AND FRAME TEST. The student is required to adjust an apparatus so that a rod appears to him to be exactly vertical even though the rod is displayed in a frame that is vividly askew.

12. IMBEDDED FIGURES TEST. The student is required to discern figures camouflaged in complex pictures, drawings, and forms.

13. Words are flashed on a screen by means of a tachistoscope. The time it requires a student to recognize emotionally neutral

words, semantically loaded words, and words artificially given emotional loading by conditioning to mild electric shock is determined both by student report and by GSR monitor.

14. The percentage of words needed for recognition as displayed by slow shutter is determined.

15. The basal GSR, blood pressure and heart rate is determined before and after several tests.

16. During tests a mild electric shock is delivered to determine the lability of the GSR, blood pressure and heart rate.

17. A number of tests are run to determine the average sensitivity threshold to electric stimulation as well as the threshold to pain by electric stimulation.

18. The average lung capacity is measured by a SPIROMETER.

19. Conditional reflexes are established and extinguished and the learning curve recorded; a) finger reflex from shock conditioned to a bell, b) GSR reflex from shock conditioned to a neutral word, c) eye blink reflex from air puff conditioned to a tone.

20. Time and number of repetitions necessary to extinguish rapid finger oscillation.

21. Time and number of repetitions necessary to extinguish rapid hand squeeze on exercisor.

22. The average hand strength is measured by a DYNAMETER.

23. The average reaction time, and time to onset of reaction is measured in a standard RT apparatus.

24. The student is blindfolded and his normal adjusting sway is recorded. Tape recorded suggestions of rocking back and forth are played and the sway is recorded and compared.

25. SPIRAL AFTEREFFECTS TEST. The student observes a disk on which is painted a spiral spinning at a constant rate. He describes his perception after the disk is stopped and the time or continuing reaction is noted.

26. Words are shown by slide projector and reactions on the polygraph are noted as are reactions to standardized pictures.

27. DIAGNOSTIC DIFFERENTIAL TEST is administered and the protocols sent blind to scorer and interpreters.

28. RORSCHACH is administered and protocols sent blind to two separate sets of analysts.

29. Quirk's modification of the WOLPE Inventory of Fears.

30. ADORNO Authoritarian Scale of Values.

31. WILLOUGHBY Inventory of Anxieties.

32. The discrepancy between a Q-Sort of self-description and parental ideal description is determined.

33. GLOVER SCALE of Sexual Values.

34.-37. Green Valley Oral Test of Logical Creativity.

38. OTIS Mental Ability.

39. OTIS Arithmetic Reasoning Test.

40. IOWA SILENT READING TEST.

41.-49. IOWA TEST OF EDUCATIONAL DEVELOPMENT (or STANFORD ACHIEVEMENT TESTS).

50. DAVIS ADVANCED READING.

51. PRELIMINARY SCHOLASTIC APTITUDE TEST.

appendix

A

AUTHOR'S INTRODUCTION
TO
PUTTING MEDICINE INTO THE "MEDICAL MODEL"
by S. D. Klotz, M.D.

For many years now something called the "medical model" has dominated the care of people described as "mentally ill." These people used to be called crazy, insane, criminal, difficult, slow, different, stupid, nasty or other words now regarded as "unprofessional" to use.

Most people think that Bedlam and snakepits were the only way in which the mad were handled before the Civil War. However, most "crazy" people were tolerated in small communities, as they are today in many parts of the world. Most insane were cared for in small hospitals (the original meaning of the word is "a refuge"). These hospitals practiced a gentle art called "moral therapy." It was kindly, supportive and aimed at returning insane people to communities as soon as possible. Their successes were much greater than mental hospital successes today even though ours are much more expensive, larger, and staffed with highly educated professionals.

The "medical model" says, in effect, this different person is different because of a disease, a trauma, an invasion. The idea that differences might be quite natural is really not entertained. Unfortunately, the "medical model" became dominated by Freudians and psychoanalysis (which is still the major point of view taught to psychiatrists). People are held in great buildings called hospitals and perhaps for an hour a day or a week they are talked to and this is called "treatment" of a "disease."

Of course, since the advent of tranquilizers the number of people in state mental hospitals has steadily declined. There are many who say that tranquilizers really reduce the anxiety of the psychiatrist and let him do what he should have done anyway. Experience in other countries tends to confirm this, as does a more recent experience in the state hospitals of New York when many "mentally ill" people were released because of a strike. Special social workers assigned after the strike had a very hard time convincing most of these people that they needed further "treatment" and no ill effects of the discharge have been demonstrated. Quite the contrary. In addition, we now see serious results in long term use of phenothiazines and other tranquilizers, ranging from strongly reduced cognitive capacity, through liver and other damage, to allergic reactions which actually cause psychoses. This process is not new in Twentieth Century psychiatry. It is not well known, but Freud was early convinced that cocaine and other narcotics were solving the problems of the "mentally ill." Apparently the climate is now right for the public to accept a new and different addicting drug as a means of managing difficult people.

There is, however, another "medical model." This "model" says all but the critically and acutely ill should be treated on an outpatient basis, living as normally as possible at home, using all of the resources of the family while a physician studies the biological dynamics of the individual. Mental hospitals used to be filled with paretic Napoleons. First, it became possible to talk about VD in public and to educate people to the dangers, and then antibiotics almost completely reduced the problem. While VD is on the rise again, we do have good diagnostics and treatments, and very few individuals suffer the disease long enough to suffer the psychoses that may result from its damage to the brain. Pellagra used to fill southern hospitals (because of poverty and regional preferences for vitamin B deficient diets).

Just requiring bread manufacturers to put niacin in their sticky product has almost completely eliminated this problem. Cretinism has responded to thyroid extracts. Other clear cut cases of serious, gross behavior and emotional problems are now a substantial part of internal medicine and of biological psychiatry.

Unfortunately, *most* psychologists and psychiatrists do not require their "patients" to have a thorough medical inventory. While their ready use of tranquilizers and stimulants is now well documented these therapists are really poorly trained and motivated to practice biological medicine. I know many psychiatrists who have not used a stethescope for years, and who will frankly admit they are not qualified to give a physical examination.

Since I am a medical layman, I have asked an extremely well qualified physician, S. D. Klotz, M.D., for permission to include his paper as an appendix to this HANDBOOK. It is an adequate introduction to some of the biological issues that grossly affect behavior. I hope it will sensitize parents and teachers, if not psychologists and psychiatrists, to seek a dedicated, persistent, *informed* internist as an absolutely critical member of the teaching/parenting team. Good schooling, and good child care cannot occur without good diet and good biological practices.

A great deal of the success of Green Valley School is based on the fact that this very busy and highly qualified physician is a compassionate healer who persists in seeking biological answers to difficult cases.

I cannot too highly recommend Dr. Klotz's book, GUIDE TO MODERN MEDICAL CARE (Scribners, 1967).

George von Hilsheimer

appendix B 9

HOW GREEN VALLEY PUTS MEDICINE
IN THE MEDICAL MODEL

Sol D. Klotz, M.D., FACA, FAAA, FASI

Green Valley School, located in Orange City, Florida, is a residential center for children in trouble. Many of their adolescents arrive there after having been in hospitals or other institutions from many different areas in the United States. The usual medical workup that accompanies them consists only of a general physical examination, confirming the absence of communicable disease, the adequacy of the heart and lungs, along with blood count and urine analysis.

The Director, Reverend George von Hilsheimer, and his staff, while primarily educators by training, have become so well oriented to the potential hazards of physical disability upon behavior that they have developed a high index of suspicion and consequently have referred to me many of their children for further medical evaluation. Surprisingly, in spite of previous medical clearance, a great deal of medical pathology was uncovered that has been of great value in the remediation of their behavioral symptoms.

In an attempt to create a model of assessment involving less expense than the full laboratory workup, Green Valley has given in-service-training to a substantial portion of its staff in order that they might monitor and objectify behavior at regular intervals following meals. Several years experience initially established that a very large number of children who seemed to be "frank" behavior problems in fact suffered a variety of physical conditions contributing to that behavior. Regular routines of single food trials, monitoring of pulse, blood pressure, respiration (both rate and quantity), and temperature as well as the basal skin resistance to electricity, and the Galvanic Skin Response, and a large battery of conditioning and perceptual tests were related to prior food intake.

Gross observations of behavior as well as these objectified measures seemed adequately to predict those individuals whom medical laboratory work would indicate as suffering two major conditions, allergies and hypoglycemia. Green Valley has substantially modified its common diet to exclude the most common foods producing allergic responses and excluding those foods regarded as incompatible with a hypoglycemic dysfunction (essentially all readily digested carbohydrates, especially all forms of sugar).

Out of 222 adolescents treated at the school during a 5 year period ending 30 June, 1968, 191 were clinically diagnosed as allergic with behavioral implications by their non-medical and para-medical staff. Twenty-one of these had thorough laboratory workups at our clinic and of these 21, all have achieved 100% remediation of academic and behavioral liabilities as control of the allergic symptoms was attained. One hundred and eighty-five were remediated of the larger group.

One hundred and seventeen of the total group were clinically diagnosed as hypoglycemics with behavioral implications by non-medical and para-medical staff. These children were followed in the Green Valley milieu for six months. At the end of that time 12 had not shown significant improvement. These 12 had *thorough* medical workups which revealed clinically significant hypoglycemia. There was 100% remediation of symptoms by strict control of diet. One adolescent had a *Cushing's syndrome* secondary to an adrenal tumor, whose removal helped in the subsequent management of this individual's behavioral problem.

It was, of course, interesting to discover that all difficult cases whose behavior had not been remediated by the milieu and reeducation process at Green Valley, and who had been assessed by nonmedical staff as very probably suffering from strong allergies or serious hypoglycemia were in fact confirmed by laboratory analysis. Closer supervision of diet, and hypodesensitization (in the case of allergies) were followed, together with routines prescribed in our clinic, with a subsequent relief of problem behaviors. It is, of course, not strictly possible to say that the medical intervention was the primary cause of remediation. However, it is extremely suggestive. It is also the opinion of the educators that these resistant cases could not have been reached by milieu therapy, reeducation or other tactics without the correction of the physical dysfunctions.

A research model is now being followed so that an equivalent number of adolescents will be given a complete laboratory screening just prior to or immediately following entrance at Green Valley. These findings will, in so far as possible, be kept "blind" and a close monitoring of various objective measures of remediation will be plotted against those of the original group.

The frequent occurrences of these physical complications in socalled frank behavioral problem cases warrants a more detailed discussion of our experience with the hope that it will guide others toward those areas of medicine that we feel should be more frequently considered and put into the medical model.

At least 85% of the children arriving at Green Valley School have been noted to have nutritional deficiency and more than 80% have allergic symptoms affecting their perception and vitality. Most of them have been living under strongly stressful conditions that cannot help but affect their physiologic functions, particularly those involving their endocrine and metabolic systems.

The effects of the endocrines on human behavior have been well documented. Both excesses and deficiencies can alter the mental and nervous functions of the individual. Excess thyroid secretion causes increased nervous activity and tone, difficulty in concentrating on any one subject long enough to carry it through to completion. There may be hallucinations, delusions and psychotic behavior. Decreased thyroid secretion leads to decreased activity and slowing of mentation. Psychoses may also occur, usually of the depressed type. In hyperparathyroidism, psychotic behavior is sometimes seen to be related to the associated hypercalcemia. In hyperparathyroidism there may be convulsive episodes resulting in mental retardation. Calcium metastasis to the brain may contribute to mental deterioration. The influence of gonadal hormones on behavior is well known. The aggressive tendencies of the male and the compliant manner of the female are to some extent dependent on their respective sex hormones. Diseases of the pancreas are frequently associated with aberrations of the blood sugar content. Lethargy and erratic behavior is often noted in patients with uncontrolled diabetes due to hyperglycemia. Lowered blood sugar levels can be associated with psychosomatic or psychotic behavior.

While blood sugar levels are primarily affected by the action of insulin, many other factors are responsible for the proper glucose homeostasis, such as the type of food intake, the rates of absorption from the intestine, deposition in the tissues, glycogenolysis particularly in the liver and muscles, gluconeogenesis from protein and insulin breakdown; also the inhibitory effect on peripheral utilization of carbohydrates and the direct effect on oxidation of fat and protein.

Hypoglycemia which follows glucose intake is usually caused by failure of the adrenocorticosteroids to inhibit insulin activity and influence the rate of insulin catabolism. A fall of the glucose level results in the activation of the hypothalamic-pituitary-adrenal system. The C. N. S., especially the hypothalamus, activates the pituitary which in turn activates an adrenal response. In pituitary failure, there is no response to insulin administration even though the rate of blood glucose fall could be sufficient to produce an adrenal response with an intact pituitary.

As we know, the human organism, and in particular the nervous system, operates for the most part on glucose which must be supplied by the blood at an appropriate concentration. The adrenal cortex, through its glucosteroids, plays a major role in regulating this concentration. It is felt by many observers that functional hypoglycemia is not a true hyperinsulinism except in rare cases of pancreatic adenoma but due to a failure of the glucosteroids to antagonize or catabolize insulin, associated with a hypoadrenocortical state. Symptoms of hypoglycemia depend upon the degree of the rate of glucose fall along with the acuteness and chronicity of its presence. Early symptoms are similar to those seen after administration of epinephrine, i.e., fainting, tremulousness, emotional disturbances, excessive perspiration, chilliness, circumoral numbness and pallor, hunger, apprehension, paresthesis, palpitation, hand tremor and degrees of mental cloudiness. As the hypoglycemia progresses, a variety of symptoms such as headache, difficulty in concentration, disorientation, mental confusion, dizziness, faintness, diplopia and coldness of extremities may develop. The patient may be unable to walk or may stagger; he may be depressed, restless and maniacal. In severe hypoglycemia, muscle twitching and generalized convulsions are followed by retrograde amnesia and unconsciousness.[3,4,5,6]

Electrolyte disturbances can alter behavior. Stress of any type augments potassium excretion by the kidneys, because of the mobilization of electrolytes from tissue cells and by sodium retention. The clinical state of potassium depletion results in paralysis or weakness with tetanic contractions of hands and legs, muscle weakness and paresthesia. The respiratory muscles are particularly susceptible with development of signs of dyspnea, cyanosis and respiratory failure. Magnesium electrolytes play a role in enzymatic functions and other physiologic processes. Hypermagnesemia results in lethargy and coma, while hypomagnesemia which must be considered in all patients with malnutrition, may produce bizarre tremors, athetotic and choreoform movements of the extremities.

The effect of changes in calcium levels was briefly discussed under symptoms of parathyroid disorders.

Neurological syndromes due to allergic hypersensitivity have been documented many times. There have been case reports describing, after the ingestion of certain foods, where individuals have developed symptoms simulating such neurological syndromes as myesthenia gravis, spinal cord syndrome, and psychomotor epilepsy. Recent observations suggest that allergic and immunological mechanisms are important in several organic neurological diseases.[7] Since Basso[8] and Goltman[9] separately observed recurrent cerebral edema due to food allergies, there has been no doubt that allergic reactions can occur in the central nervous system. Symptoms frequently reported as due to allergy are some of the headaches, migraines and convulsions usually due to foods or drugs. The convulsions may be of the petit mal or even grand mal types.

The allergic-tension-fatigue syndromes can be seen in children of all ages and also adults. It may be easily overlooked if one is not aware it can exist. Clues suggesting its presence are as follows: A pale and sallow complexion although blood tests reveal no anemia; eyes having dark circles with puffiness of skin about the eyelids; the child looks irritable, listless and tired even though he has had a full night's sleep. The parents are concerned about his sluggishness, drowsiness and lack of interest in both play and school work. There is irritability, peevishness, unhappiness and unpredictable behavior. The severity of symptoms of fatigue and nervousness vary with the individual. Occasionally, there may be more severe neurologic and psychologic signs and symptoms, including paresthenia, facial tics, severe personality disturbances and even psychotic behavior. Alternating type of symptoms are characteristic. Sleepiness on the one hand, yet insomnia on the other hand, sluggish thinking, difficulty in concentration, inability to be pleased and general unhappiness. The symptoms can best be divided into those of:

1. Motor tension (hyperkinesis) manifested by overactivity, restlessness, clumsiness, poor manual behavior, inability to relax.

2. Sensory tension manifested by irritability, oversensitivity, insomnia, photophobia, hypersensitivity to noise.

3. Motor fatigue manifested by achiness and tiredness.

4. Sensory fatigue manifested by sluggishness and torpor.

5. Less common mental and nervous symptoms may be mental depression, feeling of unreality, bizarre and irrational behavior, paranoid ideas, inability to concentrate, nervous tics and paresthesias.

The above nervous system symptoms may be associated with other systemic manifestations such as increased salivation, sweating, abdominal pain, headache and enuresis.[10]

Certain drugs, particularly psychotherapeutic medicines that behavior problem patients may be on, can cause neurologic symptoms. The tranquilizers, particularly the phenothiazines, reserpine, steroids, can cause convulsive disorders, Parkinsonism and psychoses.

Ever present chemical agents in our surroundings often are the unrecognized causes of clinical entities frequently seen by the allergist, since the reactions to chemical susceptibility may closely resemble the symptoms induced by allergies and are present in many allergic individuals. Many of the reactive chemicals that contaminate our air, water and food are derivatives or prepared from hydrocarbons of common genesis—coal, petroleum and natural gas. The victim of chemical susceptibility becomes sick from often repeated relatively small amounts of materials in non-toxic doses that have no apparent effect on other non-susceptible people who are similarly exposed.[12]

It is amazing the amount of additives derived from coal tar products that are present in pills, foods, candies, bakery products, soaps and preservatives, most of them unlabeled.

Medical Management

How can we determine if the patient may be suffering from a physical ailment that is producing or aggravating the behavior disorder? As I mentioned earlier one can by having a high index of suspicion along with an awareness that the symptoms may be due to medical disorders other than a primary behavioral disturbance in the classic sense.

When indicated, the medical workup should evaluate the thyroid function, including a P.B.I., or radioactive thyroid uptake. Electrolyte determinations of potassium, chlorides, sodium, calcium and magnesium may be indicated. When symptoms are suggestive, an oral 4-5 hour glucose tolerance test should be done to look for functional hypoglycemia. If symptoms are provoked before the 5 hour period is up, the test should be discontinued and the patient given food. Sometimes an afternoon glucose tolerance test may pick up a reactive hypoglycemia more easily.[3] When an allergic evaluation is indicated, skin tests for inhalant and food sensitivities may be performed. Food skin tests are not 100% reliable and occasionally one uses food elimination diets or provocative food tests.

Frequently, 24 hour urinary collections for 17-Ketogenic and 17-Hydroxy cortiosteroid levels should be done.

Where pathology is discovered, it should be corrected. For example, a 16 year old white female student at Green Valley School was seen because of severe obesity and some elevation of blood pressure. Menses was irregular and at times prolonged. She had a somewhat moon shaped facies, an increased amount of chin hair, a protuberant abdomen with purplish striae. Pelvic examination revealed a male escutcheon with some hypertrophy of the clitoris. Electrolyte studies were normal as were P.B.I., fasting blood sugar and skull x-rays. Twenty-four hour urines for 17-Ketosteroids and 17-Ketogenic steroids were elevated 3 times above the normal. Radiograms revealed a soft tissue mass 5x4 cm. on the right pole of the kidney, which later was confirmed by retroperitoneal air studies. At surgery, a right adrenal tumor was removed. For the first time the patient has started to lose weight with a marked change in well being and personality.

When an *impaired* glucose tolerance curve is found or one producing hypoglycemia symptoms, the patient is put on a diet that is relatively high in protein, devoid of concentrated carbohydrates and added sugar. The patient is encouraged to snack frequently during the day and at times during the night. Foods allowed are meats, fish, and shellfish, dairy products (eggs, milk, butter and cheese), milk between meals, milk, cheese, and/or butter and saltines before retiring, salted nuts, peanut butter, protein bread, Sanka, weak tea, sugar free sodas and soybeans and its products. Foods to be avoided are potatoes, corn, macaroni, spaghetti, rice, pie, cake, pastry, sugar, candies, dates and raisins, cola and other sweet soft drinks, coffee, strong tea and all hot and cold cereals.[6]

When patients are discovered to be allergic to inhalants, a program of hyposensitization injections to those inhalants is started. Definite food allergies are eliminated. Rarely in this day of abundance are attempts at food desensitization made, but occasionally we have for a particular important food item.

The medical program is of importance in the restoration and maintenance of body homeostasis, reflected by stabilizing the nutritional, hormonal and nervous function of the body. These individuals will need proper counseling to guide them in their social adjustment. But this cannot happen too easily, if at all, until the former has been achieved.

References:

1. *von Hilsheimer, George:* Personal communication of Data from Green Valley School, Orange City, Florida.

2. *von Hilsheimer, George:* Strictly for Parents—the Tom Sawyer phenomenon—some comments on Why Kids Put Jam on the Cat, Journal of Learning Disabilities 1:70. 1968.

3. *Roberts, H. J.:* Afternoon Glucose Tolerance Testing in Diabetogenic Hyperinsulinism. Clinical Research 12:44. 1964.

4. *Roberts, H. J.:* The Syndrome of Narcolepsy and Diabetogenic (Functional) Hyperinsulism, with special reference to Obesity, Diabetes, Idiopathic Edema, Cerebral Dysrhythmias and Multiple Sclerosis (200 patients). Journal American Ceritics Society 12:926. 1964.

5. *Tintera, J. W.:* Endocrine Aspects of Schizophrenia: Hypoglycemia of Hypoadrenocorticism, Journal of Schizophrenia 1:150. 1967.

6. *Tintera, J. W.:* The Hypoadrenocortical State and Its Management, New York State Journal of Medicine 55:1869. 1955.

7. *Campbell, M. Brent:* Neurological Allergy, Review of Allergy 22:80. 1968.

8. *Basso, P.:* Angioneurotic Edema of the Brain. Med. Clin. N. Amer. 16:109. Sept. 1932.

9. *Goltman, A. M.:* Mechanism of Migraine, J. Allergy 7:351. 1936.

10. *Speer, Frederic, M.D.:* The Allergic Child, Hoeber Medical Division, p. 332. 1966 ed.

11. *Kittler, Frederick J. and Ramsey, Reginold C Jr.:* The Relationship of Allergy to Cerebral Dysfunction, Southern Medical Journal 61:1039. 1968.

12. *Randolph, T. C.:* Human Ecology and Susceptibility to the Chemical Environment, Annals of Allergy 19:533. 1961.

appendix 10

HUMANITAS

There are six documents which formally describe us: a covenant, which is a poetic expression of the best that we can say about ourselves in less than forty lines;

agreements, which are those things we care to remind ourselves about our religious identity;

the discipline, which is the political organization and charter indicating the way in which we make decisions and the limits we agree to observe;

contracts, which are specific business agreements, or narrower limits we make for long term use with each other;

legal documents of incorporation and legal contracts;

and a prose statement about what we think we are, this being it.

We trace our origins to the Little Brothers of the Common Life and the Brothers of the Free Spirit, latitudinarian religious orders in the Low Countries, Bohemia, Transylvania and Poland during the 14th and 15th centuries. These orders, like us, maintained humanistic schools teaching a scientific, experimental curriculum through a discipline founded on love and self-direction rather than arbitrary authority. During the Reformation these orders became the source of the Radical Reformers—Anabaptists, Amish, Mennonites, Moravian and Hutterian Brethren, Brethren of Unity and others.

Among the Radical Reformers the Hutterians evolved as Christian communes working in the larger community as artisans, engineers, doctors, architects and technicians. Although they were persecuted they found many welcome havens because of the high quality of their education and technology. When they moved to this continent, however, they gave up their urban identity and professions to become innovative and scientific farmers in communities far removed from urban centers. Unlike the Amish and Mennonites they did not give up the labor-saving devices of science. They discarded the show and circumstances of worldly living, sharing common clothing and goods and life, and adopted austerity as a tactic in the world for capital growth and self-discipline.

There is no doubt that the removal to rural communities that almost all Hutterians followed when they came to this continent is the best guarantee of survival with intact values. However, our ancestors believed that a witness to the world and a testing of faith in the context of the world is more important than survival. Still, we recognize that our witness as a group has often been almost extinguished and that the path we have chosen risks both erosion of members and erosion of values.

Humanitas has extended the latitudinarian and noncreedal position of the Anabaptists to welcome into fellowship anyone who is willing to accept our discipline. Technically, this was possible in the past; however, we now specifically welcome other Christians, Jews, Hindus, Buddhists, Muslims, humanists and others. Representatives of all have been brothers.

We have never been "theological." The Radical Reformers went back to the New Testament as thoroughly as possible both in belief and practice. They, and we, believe that all men are capable of facing the ultimate for themselves. We do not elevate clergy to priestly status, but understand that all believers are priests. We do not build church buildings, organize Sunday schools, separate worship from the ordinary course of life, or speculate on the nature of God or the ultimate. As St. Augustine put it, "We know not what God is, but what He is not."

We think that all theological statements, all ultimate statements, are imperfections and, therefore, not to be regarded as closed. We believe that no word should stand between us and fellowship with other souls. We do believe that behavior can separate. We believe that covenanted people ought to separate themselves from those whose behavior they regard as wrong. It is wrong now, and always to take bread from a child. It is wrong now, and always to make determinations about people before having evidence. Many other absolute value statements can be made on which we behaviorally agree. Fundamentally, however, we are like the rural Hutterians, trying to build our own faith and redemption. Our witness to other people is not an attempt to convert them or even to judge them. Our separation is not a condemnation but merely an attempt to preserve what we think is right in our own lives. We believe in tribal values. We are willing to let anyone join our tribe, but we strongly distinguish between us and others. We do not buy the idea that all human life is equally of value. No one else does either, but we are quite clear in saying to those interested in joining us—this is your family, it comes first.

Most people seem to need guilt, denial and arbitrary authority. Certainly enough evidence exists to give some weight to the idea of a "death instinct." We do not see this instinct in our rural communities—longevity is extended, degenerative diseases few, neuroses, crime and social disorder unknown, the only mental illnesses are those that seem organic in origin. We are trying to build an ongoing community of love that remains engaged in the world, witnessing to life as the gift of God. Most people act as if (even when they say they don't believe in God) they still owed someone a price for their lives. We are at war with this idea and with those who insist on it.

The Christians among us believe that Jesus' sacrifice was made for all and was perfect. That is, we believe that sin and guilt are, in fact, dead. We do not believe that the preachers of guilt and sin are witnessing for Christ. They murder His sacrifice. We think that those who emphasize guilt in the world are serving evil. What is necessary is to discover how to make redemption accessible to people. We do not presume that because they have learned not to listen to the Jesus language that they are lost. It is up to us to find a way to translate, just as if they spoke Swahili.

The humanists among us think we are trying to find ways to enable people to live as fully functioning social creators. In this language we still find that guilt and the need for justification are important barriers.

The rationalizing of myth has made Christ unaccessible to people with semantic hangups. We are committed to making Christ accessible. There truly is no need for guilt, but most people live in guilt. They believe at the gut level in Satan but not in Christ. They believe in sin but not in redemption. They are shaped by demonic forces but cannot feel the Holy Spirit, the Comforter, the Redeemer.

We think that if this language puts off the rationalized modern then we are being idolatrous to insist on it. Unfortunately, there seems to be no substitute language with easy currency.

As a group we are contemptuous of the "success" of psychotherapy. This contempt is not theoretical—anything that enlarges joy and competence is from God—but is based on research and evaluation. There is no evidence that any process other than that of community, in fact, works to enlarge, sustain, preserve and make joyful human life.

We have historically been contemptuous of churches and thought those who build them idolators. Historically, we refused to maintain a separated clergy. We make our preachers earn their bread by the sweat of their noses and think those who elevate authorities are idolators.

We believe that the only faith that is real is that which makes individuals live together in peace, mutual aid, responsibility, joy, patience, love and reconciliation. We have never believed that all who called Lord, Lord were from the Master. Nor have we been concerned if, living as the Master showed, they called not on Him.

We give service to those who are not brothers for our own good. First, we have our witness to give. The Gospel, which simply means the good news, we have is that sin has no meaning, that guilt is dead. If more people can believe this then the joy that fills our living will enrich others who will enrich us. Beyond that, a world that worships sin and guilt, and believe them important, has always fought people who live in joy and reconciliation. It is to our advantage to fill the world with joy. Joy seeks joy.

It is also for our own good that we give service to those for whom these issues are really irrelevant—those about to die of hunger or pain, or so reduced by society that they have no human intellect. We learn how life is shaped and how simple the important things are. We no longer have to "find ourselves," or "come to terms with ourselves," or "find out who we really are." We are those who love and enjoy and who would not have others hungry, ugly or abused. We are those who know that when we strain for a look at God's face, He will only show us His backside. We know that we are not enough to change the entire world, but we can go about knowing that our dues are paid.

We live as a community, using austerity as a tactic for our own growth and good, because we know that we will be larger for knowing who we are, for knowing the good, for knowing we have brothers who care, who delight in us, who will feed us and our children, who will share our work, who will discipline themselves with us to the tasks we have chosen, and who will not use the discipline to resurrect guilt and sin in our lives but to enlarge joy and love.

We live as a community because assembling resources immediately gives any group with good morale, good discipline, good faith and competence a capital advantage over the isolated.

Austerity, particularly when practiced by a group in a wealthy society, immediately enlarges the capital advantage of a community. Austerity also seems to discipline the community, to prevent conflict, to increase morale, and to sharpen goals. There is nothing really mysterious or religious about it—any small businessman who hopes to grow uses the same tactic.

Austerity is a relative term. Both we and rural communities enjoy equipment advantages that our professional peers covet. We have greater security, better health and more complex vacations and hobbies that most Americans can afford.

We like to think that all of our behavior is motivated by an interest in self. If we are decent it is not for the approval of others, or even for their good. It is that we might know ourselves as men. We are always suspicious of those who come saying they want to serve God or mankind. We do not presume—it is all we can do to serve ourselves.

The way it turns out is that we have a research mandate in social engineering. Our utopian goal is to restructure society into communities that respect individual difference and support the freest expressions of individuals. As realists we are interested in what works. We forbid any research or service team to continue any particular service for more than 36 months. Even if the team believes the service would become self-directing in the 37th month, if only we would continue, we cut it off. Our idea is that if we can't make it work in that time, we don't know what we are doing, or we know what we are doing and need the people we are helping more than they need us. Since 1957 we have experimented in the following range of enterprises:

> student directed college organizations for action and cultural programs;
>
> lay directed national movements for political action, reform or cultural enrichment;
>
> lay directed local groups for self-education, family therapy and social action;
>
> locally directed social services (child care centers for migrant farm hands, youth centers, remedial reading centers, etc.);
>
> schools, treatment centers and useful innovation in teaching techniques and therapy programs;

grass roots political action in black and white slums (in the U.S. and Canada);

Our criteria for success are:

the institution must survive the following process and personnel by at least three years;

the organizational period must be no more than six months;

the technique must be 85% as effective as direct consultation when transmitted by writing or film and tape;

the institution must rely heavily on volunteers and laymen and must be directed by local people (it may hire staff);

the cost of operation must be 1/3 or less of common practice;

the program goals must be clearly and operationally defined and reached to a level substantially superior than common practice.

During a long period of our history we insisted that projects would be regarded as successful only if the personnel working in them were totally unscreened. While we no longer follow this strict practice, our screening is solely on the basis of superficial social suitability for the task—and this is largely because the research and action we now interest ourselves in is among upper middle class and upper class populations.

Our level of success by these criteria has been more than 90%.

Ideally, we would trade leadership among ourselves more frequently. Unfortunately, we are still too small to achieve ideal movement of leadership. Still, the present business manager of our school was last year academic dean, the year before dean of students, the year before a teacher and before that a camp counselor and laborer. Our present academic dean was formerly a tutor, the organizer of one of the most successful demonstrations of minimal intervention in legal reform (the national abortion law reform movement), a street worker, executive director of a sanitarium for brain anomalous infants, and organizer of one of the most successful member supported cultural institutions in the country (the subscriber supported FM stations).

Today our research and services focus on school and retaining of people in trouble—ranging from criminals to long term patients in mental hospitals. Our enterprises include schools, treatment programs for disturbed adolescents, small farms, commercial fishing, manufacture of electronics equipment for psychologists and publishing.

By 1974 we intend to establish a closed community to provide an optimum environment for families to investigate our ideas of maximizing human potential. We are talking of changing our practice of recruiting members only through the service enterprises. This would mean recruiting for people interested in community per se.

appendix

A Backword by the Author

The rough manuscript of this book was sent to several score friends and colleagues and three important opinions emerged that required some comment, amendment and reaction.

First, everyone thought that general knowledge about learning theory was too limited not to make technical comments on modes, styles, means, methods, processes and patterns of learning, particularly the hierarchy of learning in the developing child (the reader receives my apology for the technicality of comments beginning on page 10; however, they seem important to include).
clude).

Second, nearly everyone I know who works with kids is discouraged, angry, resentful, frustrated and pessimistic. By now I am a well paid lecturer for all kinds of audiences about education. When I talk to parents they tell me that the school boards are a pack of political snakes, the supervisors time-serving ex-coaches, the principals worse than useless, the teachers doing a job that beats working in an office, and other parents are horrible. When I talk to teachers they tell me how parents demand grades and grading and daily progress reports, how the principals won't let them create a rich structure of education for children, how the superintendents and school boards are basically craven and power hungry politicians and how the kids are monstrous brats. I remember with particular vividness one invitation to give a three day training workshop. I was to speak just before opening of school in one of the wealthiest school districts in America, a golden ghetto near Cleveland (*wealthier* than Shaker Heights). My thought was, "Wow, for once I'm going to be able to focus on teaching and not on reteaching and problems." How naive! All the teachers wanted to talk about was problem kids. One principal jumped up during one of my answers and shouted, "But, Reverend, you don't understand, tomorrow we're going out into the foxholes, into a real battleground out there." This, in a school with carpets in every room! When I talk to principals they tell me about the crazy parents, the lousy teachers they are stuck with, their miserable superintendent and the State Board of Education. When I meet with superintendents they tell me that I wouldn't believe the principals they get, and, of course, the State Department in *their* state is really incredible.

Once, even, I was invited to talk to all of the professionals in education who work at the State Department of Education (in Connecticut). After I had finished a pretty long talk the Commissioner was very enthusiastic about what I had said and told the rest, "This is what I've been telling you all along." During the discussion, however, one Department head said "But, Reverend, you don't understand, *The Establishment,* the powers behind the throne, won't let us do it that way." Believe me, having worked in New York State, and for several years in New York City I do know the depths of venality to which school administrators can sink. But I don't believe this is true for the whole country, nor for the majority of schools and educators. The response I receive to most speeches is enthusiastic, my books and pamphlets and teaching materials sell well, and most visitors to our schools are ecstatic.

Still, a univeral opinion exists among critics of schools who differ as widely as the Rafferty Rickovers and the Holt Kohls: Teachers don't care. Principals are psychotic. School rules were made for the convenience of administrators and you can't change them. Children are victims of laziness, venality, politics, Marxism, and psychosis. True, true and true, again. But you, dear reader, and I, are not made of such stuff. We love our children. We will fight for them. We will do social work on our own (and we don't think social work is talking to kids, but getting them food, clothes, shelter, eye glasses, medical care, and love). If the school has a rule that the child can't be touched we will break the rule, get it changed, move to another district or shoot the school board chairman. We think nothing of spending two or three hundred dollars out of our own pockets to help our kids. We go out and embarrass the JayCees, the Kiwanis, the Civitans, the Christians, Jews and anyone else we can think of to get better facilities, volunteers, materials, and a richer structure for our kids. You and I are not like those people.

Third (and I have to say that this opinion of my friends and colleagues is buttressed by my own experience), is that many physicians are not worthy of the name, are not conscientious, are poorly trained, don't read, and they treat their overcharged patients with contempt. When I read that the average physician's income has *increased* as much as the average American's *total* income in the last eight years, my blood boils. I could regale you with many cases of horror about doctors, but, I think you will have your own horrible experiences and tales and don't need mine.

Hiring a psychiatrist when children are malnourished (and millions are—we have seen scores of wealthy and middle class children who are malnourished) makes less sense than hiring an astrologer. Neurologists are often barely better than psychiatrists for they, too, have been seduced by the Freudian heresy and generally *blame* the patient (or his mother), particularly if the patient is female or adolescent. If a doctor tells you the problem is "emotional" get another doctor. Unfortunately, many GP's and Internists have been seduced by the general Freudian mysticism and don't do their home or office work. If your physician will not talk to you about your illness, its causes, its course and complexities, find another physician.

You should, of course, be willing to spend extra money for the extra time a good internist or allergist or general practitioner spends with you. But, if the man is not current with his reading, if he has not kept up with the literature, if he is contemptuous of you as a human being, you have no business seeing him.

If you are told vague things like, "the problem is emotional," "well, it's a brain syndrome," or "well, maybe you have multiple sclerosis, come back in four months and we'll see what has happened," I suggest you hire another doctor. If your disorder is so complex or unusual that a good internist, backed up by a good laboratory and consultants cannot discover the trouble and prescribe a course of treatment, he ought to have the guts to tell you, "I don't know." If he does tell you "I don't know" and he is a physician, he will be seeing you frequently trying everything the vast medical literature suggests to him, and he will not give up or tell you "let's just wait and see." Or, it's emotional. Bah!

If you must have a psychiatrist we suggest you write to the American Association for Behavior Therapy, 415 East 52nd Street, New York, N.Y. 10022, for a list of members in your area. This is not an accrediting body, but it is committed to a point of view which in general believes that any behavioral or emotional problem must be solved in six months or less, or either it is not in fact an emotional problem, or we don't know how to solve it. There are, of course, those few individuals (and some countries "miraculously" have a mere fraction of what American psychiatrists regard as the irreducible minimum) whose disorders are so severe that they are a danger to themselves and others and they simply have to be put away. It is a great deal more honest and therapeutic for a doctor to have the guts to tell you that simple fact than to tell you that a "treatment" may take 15 years!

I cannot too strongly emphasize the importance of a *medical* doctor to effective education for both the normal and the difficult child (and what child is never difficult?). Nor can I too strongly emphasize the importance of a *medical* doctor for the well being of the whole family. A regular, routine, annual biological inventory that thoroughly studies the metabolism of every member of the whole family, under the direction of a qualified internist or a general practitioner will be the most important life insurance, in every sense of the term, that you can buy.

bibliography

Ashton-Warner, Sylvia, TEACHER, Simon and Schuster, New York, 1963

Astrup, Christian, PAVLOVIAN PSYCHIATRY, Charles Thomas, Springfield, Ill., 1965

Bazely, E. T., HOMER LANE AND THE LITTLE COMMONWEALTH, Schocken, New York, 1969

Beck, Joan, HOW TO RAISE A BRIGHTER CHILD, Trident, New York, 1967

Burn, M., MR. LYWARD'S ANSWER, Hamish Hamilton, London, 1956

Chall, J., LEARNING TO READ, McGraw, New York, 1967

Coleman, James, ADOLESCENTS AND THE SCHOOLS, Basic Books, New York, 1965

Engleman, S. & T., GIVE YOUR CHILD A SUPERIOR MIND, Simon & Schuster, New York, 1966

Friedenberg, Edgar, COMING OF AGE IN AMERICA, Random, New York, 1965
    DIGNITY OF YOUTH AND OTHER ATAVISMS, Beacon Press, Boston, 1965

Denison, George, LIVES OF CHILDREN, Random, New York, 1969

Franks, Cyril, CONDITIONING TECHNIQUES, Springer Publications, New York, 1964

George, W., THE JUNIOR REPUBLIC, D. Appleton and Company, New York, 1909

Ginott, Haim, BETWEEN PARENT AND CHILD, MacMillan, New York, 1965

Goffman, E., ASYLUMS, Doubleday, Garden City, New York, 1961

Goodman, Paul, GROWING UP ABSURD, Random, New York, 1960
    UTOPIAN ESSAYS, Random, New York, 1962
    COMMUNITY OF SCHOLARS, Random, New York, 1962

Hemmings, J., TEACH THEM TO LIVE, Longmans, Gram, & Co., New York, 1957

Holmes, G., THE IDIOT TEACHER, Faber and Faber, London, 1952

Holt, John, HOW CHILDREN FAIL, Pitman, New York, 1964
    HOW CHILDREN LEARN, Pitman, New York, 1969
    THE UNDERACHIEVING SCHOOL, Pitman, New York, 1969

Ilg & Ames, SCHOOL READINESS, Holt, Rinehart, & Winston, New York, 1965

Illingsworth & Illingsworth, LESSONS FROM CHILDHOOD, Livingston, London, 1966

Jones, H., RELUCTANT REBELS, Tavistock Publications, London, 1960

Klotz, S., GUIDE TO MODERN MEDICAL CARE, Scribners, New York, 1967

Kozel, J., DEATH AT AN EARLY AGE, Bantam, New York, 1968

Kohl, H., THE OPEN CLASSROOM, New York Review, New York, 1969
    TEACHING THE UNTEACHABLE, New York Review, New York, 1969
    36 CHILDREN, World Publishers, 1967

262

Koerner, James, THE MISEDUCATION OF AMERICAN TEACHERS, Pelican, New York, 1965

Krumholz and Thorensen, BEHAVIORAL COUNSELING: CASES AND TECHNIQUES, Holt, Rinehart, & Winston, New York, 1966

Lane, Homer, TALKS TO PARENTS AND TEACHERS, Schocken, New York, 1969

London, Perry, BEHAVIOR CONTROL, Harper and Row, New York, 1969
MODES AND MORALS IN PSYCHOTHERAPY, Holt, Rinehart & Winston, New York, 1964

MacKenzie, R., THE SINS OF THE CHILDREN, Collins, London, 1965
ESCAPE FROM THE CHILDREN, Collins, London, 1965
A QUESTION OF LIVING, Collins, London, 1963

Neill, A. S., SUMMERHILL: A RADICAL APPROACH TO CHILD REARING, Hart, New York, 1960
FREEDOM: NOT LICENSE, Hart, New York, 1967

Mararenko, A., ROAD TO LIFE, Foreign Language Publications, Moscow, 1951
A BOOK FOR PARENTS, FLP, Moscow, 1953
LEARNING TO LIVE, FLP, Moscow, 1953

Pearse & Crocker, THE PECKHAM EXPERIMENT, Allen & Unwin, London, 1947

Renfield, R., IF TEACHERS WERE FREE, Acropolis, Washington, D.C., 1969

Richardson, Elwyn, IN THE EARLY WORLD, Pantheon, New York, 1969

Salter, A., CONDITIONED REFLEX THERAPY, Capricorn Books, New York, 1961

Scrimshaw and Gordon, MALNUTRITION, LEARNING, AND BEHAVIOR, MIT, Cambridge, 1968

Spiel, Oskar, DISCIPLINE WITHOUT PUNISHMENT, Faber and Faber, London, 1962

Ullman & Krasner, CASE STUDIES IN BEHAVIOR MODIFICATION, Holt, Rinehart, and Winston, New York, 1965
A PSYCHOLOGICAL APPROACH TO ABNORMAL BEHAVIOR, Prentice Hall, Englewood, 1969

von Hilsheimer, G., IS THERE A SCIENCE OF BEHAVIOR, Humanities Curriculum, Orange City, Florida, 1967

Watson, J. B., BEHAVIORISM, Phoenix, University of Chicago, 1963

Wills, David, THROW AWAY THY ROD, Internl. Publications Service, New York, 1960
HOMER LANE: A BIOGRAPHY, Fernhill, New York, 1964

Wolpe & Renya, BEHAVIOR THERAPY AND EXPERIMENTAL PSYCHIATRY, Pergamon, New York, 1969

Wolpe, Salter, Renya, THE CONDITIONING THERAPIES, Holt, Rinehart, & Winston, New York, 1965

Wolpe, J., PSYCHOTHERAPY BY RECIPRICAL INHIBITION, Stanford University Press, California, 1958
THE PRACTICE OF BEHAVIOR THERAPY, Pergamon, New York, 1969

index

268

"Children need to be touched. Infants cannot go about their biological task of differentiating nerve endings, sophisticating perceptions and movements, without the assistance of a great deal of touching by others. In most families with difficult children, touching is limited to bare essentials. . . ."

—George von Hilsheimer